BRAIN LATERALITY

Brain Laterality answers one of the major questions we ask ourselves every day: where? The book provides a thematic, comprehensive overview of the brain mechanisms that influence whether we go to the left or right, on which side we stand, and which hand we use.

Covering a broad range of topics, including handedness, apraxia, and motor control, alongside theories of emotion, creativity, and genetics, the book condenses a vast amount of research from multiple fields into a concise and entertaining read.

Featuring anecdotes from the author's own illustrious research and clinical career, this book is a must-read for psychology students, neuropsychologists, neurologists, and anyone interested in the brain's role in handedness, directional movement, intention, action, and posturing.

Kenneth M. Heilman is a Distinguished Professor Emeritus in the Department of Neurology at the University of Florida and a staff neurologist at the Gainesville Veterans Affairs Medical Center. He has been the author, co-author, and editor of 20 books, more than 670 journal articles, and 115 chapters, as well as being honored by many neuropsychology and neurology organizations.

BRAIN LATERALITY

RIGHT, UP, AND FORWARD

Kenneth M. Heilman

Routledge
Taylor & Francis Group

NEW YORK AND LONDON

First published 2022
by Routledge
605 Third Avenue, New York, NY 10158

and by Routledge
2 Park Square, Milton Park, Abingdon, Oxon OX14 4RN

Routledge is an imprint of the Taylor & Francis Group, an informa business

Library of Congress Cataloging-in-Publication Data
A catalog record for this title has been requested

ISBN: 978-1-03207-392-7 (hbk)
ISBN: 978-1-03207-391-0 (pbk)
ISBN: 978-1-00320-668-2 (ebk)

DOI: 10.4324/9781003206682

Typeset in Bembo
by Newgen Publishing UK

CONTENTS

INTRODUCTION

Throughout our lives we have to ask ourselves three major questions, where, when, and how? This book discusses some of the brain mechanisms that might help us decide "where."

The Hebrew Bible has many references to the right hand and right side. For example, Exodus 15:6 states, "Your right hand, O LORD, is majestic in power, Your right hand, O LORD, shatters the enemy." Psalm 16:11 states, "You will make known to me the path of life; In Your presence is fullness of joy; In Your right hand there are pleasures forever," and Psalm 48:10 states, "As is Your name, O God, So is Your praise to the ends of the earth; Your right hand is full of righteousness."

This rightward bias is also incorporated into Christianity. The New Testament has many sections that also mention the importance of the right hand and being on the right side. For example, *Hebrews* 12:2 states, "fixing our eyes on Jesus, the author and perfecter of faith, who for the joy set before Him endured the cross, despising the shame, and has sat down at the right hand of the throne of God" and *Acts* 5:31states, "He is the one whom God exalted to His right hand as a Prince and a Savior, to grant repentance to Israel, and forgiveness of sins."

There are many other writings in both the Hebrew Bible and the New Testament that mention the right hand and on the right side. In contrast, there is little about the left hand or left side.

One of the most interesting and perplexing biblical stories about handedness and sidedness is in Genesis 48. When Joseph was told, "Your father is ill," he took his two sons Manasseh and Ephraim along with him to see Jacob. When Jacob was told, "Your son Joseph has come to you," he rallied his strength and sat up on the bed. Jacob said to Joseph, "God Almighty appeared to me in the land of Canaan, and there he blessed me and said to me, 'I am going to make you fruitful and increase your numbers. I will make you a community of peoples, and I will give this land as an everlasting possession to your descendants after you.'"

DOI: 10.4324/9781003206682-1

When Jacob saw the sons of Joseph, he asked, "Who are these?"

"They are the sons God has given me here," Joseph said to his father.

Then Jacob said, "Bring them to me so I may bless them."

Jacob's eyes were failing because of old age, and he could hardly see. So Joseph brought his sons close to him, and his father kissed them and embraced them. Jacob said to Joseph, "I never expected to see your face again, and now God has allowed me to see your children too."

Then Joseph removed them from Jacob's knees and bowed down with his face to the ground. And Joseph took both of them, Ephraim on his right toward Jacob's left hand and Manasseh on his left toward Israel's right hand, and brought them close to him. But Jacob reached out his right hand and put it on Ephraim's head, though he was the younger, and crossing his arms, he put his left hand on Manasseh's head, even though Manasseh was the firstborn.

Then he blessed Joseph and said, "May the God before whom my fathers Abraham and Isaac walked faithfully, the God who has been my shepherd all my life to this day, the Angel who has delivered me from all harm, may he bless these boys. May they be called by my name and the names of my father's Abraham and Isaac, and may they increase greatly on the earth."

When Joseph saw his father placing his right hand on Ephraim's head he was displeased; so he took hold of his father's hand to move it from Ephraim's head to Manasseh's head. Joseph said to him, "No, my father, this one is the firstborn; put your right hand on his head." But his father refused and said, "I know, my son, I know. He too will become a people, and he too will become great. Nevertheless, his younger brother will be greater than he, and his descendants will become a group of nations."

I do not know the reason for this biblical and religious right–left metaphorical dichotomy. The term "right" not only means on the side opposite the heart, but also refers to many positive attributes such as correct, good, proper, suitable, straight, and genuine-real. In contrast, the scientific term for being on the left side or being left-handed is "sinistral." The word sinister means, unfavorable, unlucky, fraudulent, and even evil. Although many people believe that the bible is the word of G-D, it was transcribed and/or written by humans and in this book, we will explore some possible reasons for this rightward bias.

I recently heard my rabbi speak about this portion of Genesis. When I came home and tried to carefully read this portion, I thought I was getting right–left confusion, a disorder that can be caused by injury to our left parietal lobe, but then I realized that I am writing this book to help others possibly understand this right-ward bias, found in the Bible, and in many other writings, as well as in other non-Judeo-Christian cultures. For example, in some Native North American cultures, the right hand represents the high, the brave, and liberty. The left hand represents destruction and death.

In the next section, I will discuss the possible brain mechanisms that might account for the biblical and cultural bias for the rightward horizontal bias, including the right hand as well as the rightward spatial bias.

In addition to the horizontal right–left directional dichotomy of action and attentional biases, there are two other directions to which we can attend and to which we can act. There are also vertical biases, up–down, of action and attention, as well as radial, forward, and backward. In the subsequent chapters, the possible brain mechanisms that might account for these biases will also be discussed.

1
RIGHT AND LEFT

Knowing Left from Right

One of the most frequent decisions we make during our entire life is choosing between left and right. We make this decision when we use our hands and arms. We also make this decision when we are looking for something, or going somewhere when walking or driving. All humans and all animals interact with other objects in space as well as their own body and other people's body. The first step in any interaction is the need to allocate attention to that object, by directing spatial attention and then perceiving the object and knowing its meaning. When needed or desired, we can then perform an action upon or with this object.

The direction of attention and movements in space can only take place in three body- centered directions, lateral-horizontal (right versus left), vertical (up versus down), and radial (forward versus backward). In this chapter, we are focusing on lateral, right and left. Right–left laterality can be both egocentric (body-head centered) and allocentric (object centered). For example, the letter "C" can appear at the beginning or end of a sentence. If the center of the book is directly in front of the reader, and the C is at the beginning of the first sentence in this book, it will be egocentrically (body-head centered) on the left side. However, independent of location in the sentence, the opening in the letter C is allocentrically (object centered) on the right. Many of the spatial behaviors and cognitive activities performed by animals and humans are right versus left lateralized, and the selection of right- versus left-lateralized actions is determined by neuronal networks in our brain. As will be discussed, different portions of the brain are important for mediating allocentric (object- centered) and egocentric (body-centered) attention.

While eating a lobster, after I finished eating the tail, I looked over the claws and was getting ready to crush the shell and start eating the meat in the claws, which has sweeter meat than does the tail; I noticed that the two claws were different in size

DOI: 10.4324/9781003206682-2

and shape. The larger of the two claws is called the "crusher claw" and the smaller claw is called the "pincer." The larger crusher claw was on this lobster's right side. I wondered if most lobsters have their crusher claw on their right side. I looked this up and read that 50% have the crusher on the right and 50% have their crusher claw on their left.

Although lobsters are unlike humans, who do have a strong hand asymmetry, lobsters as well as almost all animals have a body and/or action asymmetry. Why do we and other animals have this asymmetry?

If you build a wall that is symmetrical and has two holes with one hole on the left side and the other on the right side and these holes have the same size and shape, and while an animal is watching, you put food into one of these holes, what will this animal do? Even though the food cannot be seen from the outside, almost any hungry animal will have no trouble going to the correct hole, finding, and then eating this food. Since the wall and holes are symmetrical, how can the animal know if the food is in the hole on the right versus left side?

I do not know about lobsters, but almost all mammals can find this hole, because all animals like humans have asymmetries. These asymmetries of the self can help the human and animal localize the right and left sides of their body as well as the left and right sides of space. For example, many animals have a paw preference, and this may allow them to know one side from the other. In humans, it is often handedness that allows us to correctly navigate and know right from left. I recall when I was a young boy, a teacher asked me, "Kenny, in which hand am I holding the chalk." She was holding the chalk in her left hand. I answered, "I think you are holding the chalk in your left hand." But how did I know this. My brother Fred would play ball with me and he know that I threw the ball much better with my right than left hand and so he told me, "Kenny just throw with your right hand. You are right-handed." This was fine with me because it felt so much more natural to throw with my right hand. Therefore, when the teacher asked me this question, I threw a ball in my mind and used my right hand. I therefore knew which hand was my right hand. Since she was facing me, I knew that she was holding this chalk in her left hand. I finally answered one of her questions correctly and she said, "That is right. I mean correct. I hope you were not guessing."

What Is Handedness?

The *Merriam-Webster* defines handedness as "a tendency to use one hand rather than the other" and the *British Dictionary* defines handedness as "a preference for using one hand as opposed to the other." Thus, on the basis of hand use or hand preference, we divide humans into right-handers, left-handers, and people without a preference to use one hand more than another, called ambidextrous. As defined in these dictionaries, for the most part, people determine their handedness by the hand they most often select to perform tasks that require the use of one hand or arm or the hand that performs the most critical element of an action that requires both hands.

Most studies have revealed about 90% of people are right-handed and the remainder are left-handed or ambidextrous. However, as we will discuss, the hand a person selects to use is often dependent on the type of action they are performing. Although about 90% of people are right-handed, it is not entirely clear what produces this asymmetry. According to Darwin's evolutionary hypothesis, survival of the fittest, there must have been some survival advantage to being right-handed, but it is not clear what this might have been. One speculative hypothesis has to do with spears and shields. If you were right-handed, you would carry the spear in your right hand and the shield in your left hand. In contrast, if you were left-handed, you would carry the spear in your left hand and shield in the right hand. The human heart is almost always on the left side of the chest. Therefore, carrying the shield with the left hand would be more likely to protect the heart, and during battle, it would be likely that left-handed fighters would be more likely to be killed than those who are right-handed. Unfortunately, this explanation would be very difficult to prove and has many flaws, but I know of no other valid and proven explanations.

There has been an enormous amount of research that has attempted to help us better understand the mechanisms that determine hand preference. However, the brain mechanisms that account for handedness are very complex and still not fully understood.

Crossed Control

The human brain has two hemispheres, a right and left. Each hemisphere is divided into four major lobes: frontal, temporal, parietal, and occipital (Figure 1.1). At the very back (posterior) portion of the frontal lobes, in each hemisphere, is an area called the motor cortex (Figure 1.2).

When a person wants to move their hand, they activate the nerves cells in their motor cortex hand area (Figure 1.2). These nerve cells in this area send their axons (cables) down through the cerebral hemispheres, through the brain stem, and end in the spinal cord. The spinal cord has neurons that send their axons to the muscles that control our movement, and these corticospinal neurons activate these motor neurons in the spinal cord. For control of the upper limb, most of these spinal cord motor neurons are in the cervical (neck) portion of the spinal cord and they carry the neuronal messages to the muscles that control the arm, forearm, hand, and fingers. Before these corticospinal axons reach the spinal cord, in the brain stem (medulla), they cross to the opposite side (Figure 1.3). Therefore, the right hemisphere primarily controls the left arm and hand and the left hemisphere controls the right hand and arm.

The motor cortex is controlled and excited by areas immediately in front of the motor cortex. These areas are called the premotor cortex (Figure 1.4). The premotor cortex does receive some information from the opposite hemisphere by a large cable that connects the two hemispheres, called the corpus callosum

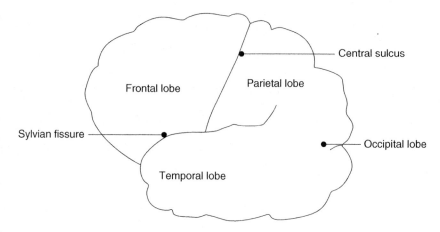

FIGURE 1.1 The Four Major Lobes of Human's Cerebral Cortex

The human cerebral cortex has four major sections called lobes. The most anterior (forward), not surprisingly, is called the frontal lobe. The lobe just behind the frontal lobe is called the parietal lobe. Below the lower portion of the posterior (back) portion of the frontal and the anterior portion of the parietal lobe is the temporal lobe. Behind the posterior sections of the parietal and temporal lobe is the occipital lobe.

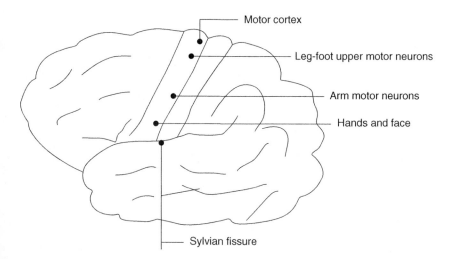

FIGURE 1.2 The Motor Cortex

The motor cortex, which is at the back end of the frontal lobes, contains the motor neurons that control our movements. These neurons send fibers to the spinal cord, and to the brain stem. The neurons going to the spinal cord are important for activating and controlling limb movements and those going to the brain stem control muscles in the face. The neurons in the motor cortex that control the legs are toward top, the arm and hand in the middle, and those that control the face are on the bottom closest the large fissure that separates the temporal lobe from the frontal and parietal lobes. This fissure is called the Sylvian fissure.

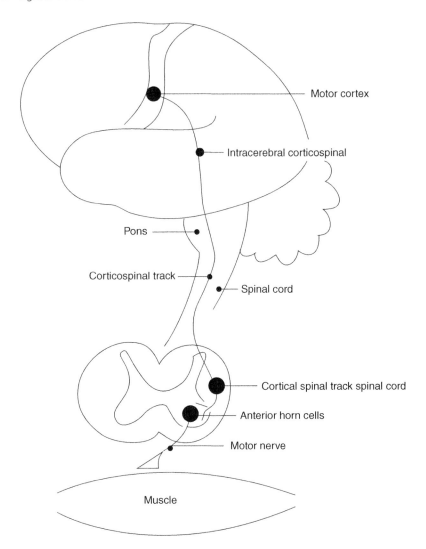

FIGURE 1.3 The Corticospinal Tract

The neurons in the motor cortex (Figures 1.2) send their cables, called axons, down to the bottom of the brain. This part of the brain is called the pons and medulla. In the medulla, most of the cortical spinal tract crosses over to the other side and then goes down to the spinal cord. With this crossing, it is the motor cortex on the left side that controls the right arm and leg and the motor cortex on the right side that controls the left arm and leg.

(Figures 1.5 and 1.6). However, this premotor cortex in each hemisphere has the strongest connections with the networks in the same hemisphere. Thus, a person's preference to use one hand rather than the other may strongly depend on the information stored in that hemisphere.

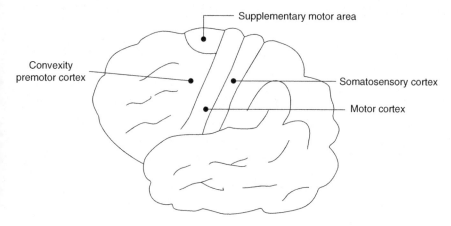

FIGURE 1.4 The Premotor Cortex

There are two areas in each hemisphere that are considered as the premotor cortex. The convexity premotor cortex is immediately in front of the motor cortex. The supplementary motor area is higher up in each hemisphere.

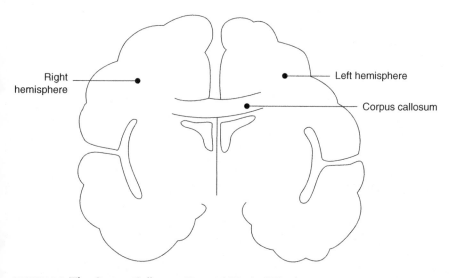

FIGURE 1.5 The Corpus Callosum (Coronal-Vertical View)

The brain has two hemispheres. Each hemisphere stores different forms of knowledge and has different processing networks. The two hemispheres are connected by the corpus callosum. This large connection permits the interhemispheric transfer of information and can also excite or inhibit the functions of the other hemisphere. In this view (Figure 1.6), the brain is cut vertically, in the middle, from the left to right side. The corpus callosum, above the lateral ventricles, is in the center and is connecting the right and left hemispheres.

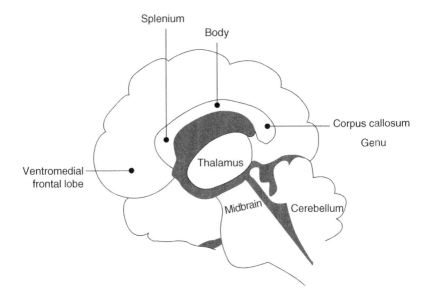

FIGURE 1.6 The Corpus Callosum (Sagittal-Longitudinal View)

Figure 1.5 shows a coronal-vertical section, where the brain is cut in middle from left to right. This figure is a sagittal section, cut in the middle of the brain between the two hemispheres, from the front to the back. This figure shows the length of the corpus callosum. The middle of the corpus callosum is called the body; the front end is called the genu; and the back the splenium. Each section carries information from the portion of the hemisphere with which it is aligned. Therefore, the anterior (front) part of the corpus callosum carries information between the frontal lobes; the more posterior part or the body carries information from the parietal lobes; and the posterior portion carries information from the occipital lobes.

Hemispheric Laterality of Language and Hand Preference

Franz Joseph Gall (1758–1828), a productive neuroanatomist and a physiologist, is best known as the founder of phrenology. Gall put forth three major hypotheses about the brain's function, organization, and anatomy including: 1) the human brain is organized in a modular fashion with different anatomic networks mediating different functions, and 2) the larger and better developed the module, the better this network can function. Gall's third hypothesis was that the shape of the brain determines the shape of the skull. Therefore, Gall thought that measurements of the skull could determine a person's attributes, which is the basic hypothesis of phrenology. Now we have several means of learning about the relationship of brain anatomy and function, using techniques such as functional magnetic resonance imaging (fMRI), positron emission tomography, and electroencephalography (EEG). Gall thought that skull measurement could reveal the size of portions of the brain. Unfortunately, phrenology became a pseudoscience, where many claims were made without the scientific evidence to support the claims. However, the shape of the brain does influence the shape of the skull, but phrenologists made claims that were not tested.

Areas of the brain that are important for mediating language, as well as many other factors, make the two hemispheres asymmetrical. With the advent of computed tomography (CT), which could reveal the shape of the brain and skull, LeMay (1977) revealed that there were asymmetries of the skull that were related to handedness and language laterality.

Paul Broca, who had a great interest in anthropology, attended a lecture by Aubertin, one of Gall's disciples. In that lecture, Aubertin proposed that the frontal lobes were important for the production of speech. Paul Broca had a patient who was admitted to a hospital in Paris for a terrible infection, and who had previously had lost his ability to speak but maintained his ability to understand other people's speech. After this patient died, Broca (1861) found on post mortem examination that this man had a cerebral lesion that was primarily located in his lower (inferior) part of the frontal lobe in his left hemisphere (Figure 1.7). In an important subsequent article, Broca (1865) reported eight right-handed patients who were aphasic and all these patients had injury to their left hemisphere. This report provided strong support for the postulate of modularity, that certain specific areas of the brain perform certain functions not performed by other parts of the brain and that the left hemisphere, in right-handed people, mediates language. In addition, since the left hemisphere controls the right hand and mediates language, based on this report and subsequent studies, it was posited that hand preference is related to hemispheric dominance for mediating language (Broca, 1865).

Language is important not only for communication between people but also for hearing and understanding external as well as internal directions that guide our actions. Therefore, the left hemisphere motor networks that control the right arm have more direct access to the language representations stored in the left hemisphere that can guide these actions. Since G-D performs meaningful actions, writers of the Bible may have used anthropometric reasoning, and that like humans God's right hand would be dominant for performing meaningful activities. In addition, when performing activities, right-handed people perform better when they use their hand on their right than left side.

Patients with epilepsy, which spreads from one hemisphere to the other and cannot be controlled with medicine, have been treated with sectioning of their corpus callosum. The corpus callosum is a large cable that connects the right and left hemispheres and has axons of neurons that go from the left hemisphere to the right hemisphere and vice versa. After this surgery, some of these patients feel that they no longer have control of their left hand. Thus, this hand has been called an "alien hand." For example, I examined a woman who had a surgical callosal disconnection to help control her seizures. She told me about an episode when she was getting dressed. She opened her closet door with her right hand and selected a dress. With her right hand, she took this dress out of her closet and laid it on a chair. Then

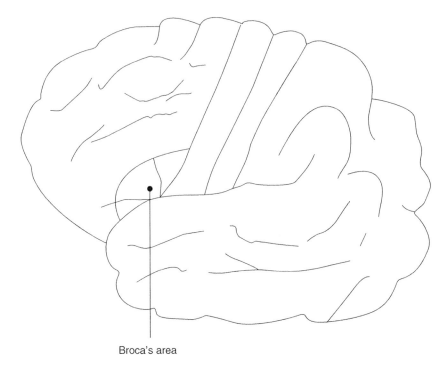

Broca's area

FIGURE 1.7 Broca's Area

The patient described by Paul Broca had a larger lesion that is shown in this figure. In addition to injuries of the left inferior frontal lobe, showed in this figure, Boca's patient had injury to a portion of the superior temporal lobe and even the anterior portion of his parietal lobe.

with her right hand, she reached and picked up a pair of shoes that matched this dress. However, her left hand pulled these shoes out of her right hand and picked up another pair of shoes. Because she did not want to wear the shoes being held in her left hand, she had her right hand remove these shoes from her left hand and dropped these shoes on the floor. With her right hand, she then again picked up the pair that she thought best matched her dress. As she was doing this, her left hand slammed the closet door against her right hand.

Because these patient's right and left hands appear to be fighting, this disorder has also been called diagonistic apraxia (Akelaitis, 1945). This woman told me that her right hand was performing her intended actions, and that she had no control of her left hand and this hand seemed to have a mind of its own. Although people with an intact corpus callosum can control their left hand, it is possible that we more often select using the right hand because when we are young and our corpus callosum is not fully formed, we might learn the right hand is more likely to carry out our intended actions.

When I was a young boy, about the age of four or five, I received a gift of a wind-up train. This locomotive had a spring inside that when wound up with a key would be able to travel a good distance. I was playing with my train in a garden that was next to the apartment house where I lived. One day after I wound up my train and it traveled. I wanted to wind it up again, but I could not find the key. I looked all over this yard and still could not find it. I loved my train and felt terrible about losing this key. We lived on the third floor of this apartment building and I went upstairs to tell my mother about losing my key. After I walked into the apartment, my mother saw how sad I looked and she asked, "What's wrong Kenny?" As I was telling her that I lost the key, I extended both my arms at the elbows and shoulders and opened my hands. The key that I had been looking for fell out of my left hand.

No, I did not have surgery on my brain, and I was a healthy five-year-old. However, research has shown that the corpus callosum does not fully mature until about the age of puberty and when I was four or five years old my callosum was not fully connected. As a boy growing up in Brooklyn, I certainly had many fights, but fortunately, none was between my right and left hands, and therefore, there was probably some interhemispheric connectivity.

Although there is much evidence that the hemispheric laterality of language influences hand preference, there is also evidence that it cannot entirely account for handedness. Studies have revealed that in about 95 percent of right-handed people it is their left hemisphere that is dominant for mediating language. However, in about 75 percent of left-handers it is their left hemisphere that is also dominant for mediating language.

Several years ago, I examined a patient who had a stroke and was aphasic. Whereas she could comprehend my speech, she had trouble expressing herself and often was only able to respond with one-word answers. This patient also had trouble naming objects and repeating sentences. In many respects, this patient's language deficits were similar to those first described by Paul Broca. The patient, however, had weakness of her left upper extremity. When I asked her if she was left-handed, she said, "No! Right hander." Many patients with aphasia also have what has been called left-right confusion and I thought she also might have this disorder. I therefore randomly elevated either my right or left hand and asked her to name the hand I elevated. I also pointed to her right or left hand and asked her to name the hand to which I pointed. Her responses were flawless. During this examination, her husband entered the room and I also asked him, "Is your wife left-handed?"

He shook his head and said, "No, she is strongly right-handed."

This patient is not the only right-hander that became aphasic from a right hemisphere stroke. Although there have been other reports, this is rarely seen. However, these right-handed patients that become aphasic with a right hemisphere lesion and the left-handed people whose left hemisphere mediates language provide evidence that the laterality of language is not the only factor that determines handedness and there must be other factors that influence handedness.

Precision of Movements

If you ask people who are right handed, why they more often use their right than their left hand, they will often tell you, "because it works better."

The human hand and fingers can make very precise-accurate, independent, and coordinated finger movements. This allows them to successfully complete many actions that are dependent on finger and hand deftness-dexterity. One of the stories that I like to tell is an event that happened when I was a behavioral neurology fellow at the Harvard Neurological Unit. The Chair of this unit was Professor Norman Geschwind. One day I was walking down the hall with Dr. Geschwind. We saw one of our neurosurgeons walking down the hallway in the opposite direction. On his forehead, he was wearing a pair of goggles. Dr. Geschwind stopped this neurosurgeon and asked him, "What are the goggles for?"

The surgeon said, "They are magnifying glasses."

Geschwind asked him, "Why did you need magnifying glasses?"

The neurosurgeon replied. "They help me to see what I am doing. Surgeons now frequently using magnification. It helps their accuracy."

After Geschwind thanked him for explaining and we again started to walk down the hallway, and he said to me, "Isn't amazing that our hand and fingers can make such precise movements that the surgeon needs a magnifying glass to provide visual feedback."

Many studies have revealed that in right-handers the right hand can perform deft-dexterous movements better the left hand. The reason for the right hand's ability to perform precise, independent but coordinated finger movements is still not entirely known. However, in the early part of the twentieth century, Hugo Liepmann (1920) noticed that right-handed people who have a left hemisphere injury lost their ability to perform precise independent finger movements of not only their contralateral right hand but also their left hand. He called this disorder limb-kinetic apraxia. Later we reported a right-handed man who had a loss of connectivity between the two hemispheres, from a lesion in his corpus callosum (Acosta, Bennett & Heilman, 2014). This man maintained his ability to perform deft movements of his right hand, but not his left hand, suggesting that it was his left hemisphere that has important role in the programing the deft movements of both hands.

In the back portion of the frontal lobes, there is an area called the primary motor cortex (Figure 1.2). This area of the cortex contains motor neurons. These motor neurons have long branches (axons) that travel down through the hemispheres, into the brain stem and then down into the spinal cord until they reach the neurons that are in the spinal cord, called lower motor neurons. These lower motor neurons go to the muscles in the arm and hand. They are responsible for bringing the signals to the muscles that make them contract (Figure 1.3).

One possible explanation of the superior deftness-dexterity of the right hand is that there are more neurons in the motor cortex of the left than right hemisphere of right-handers and that the area of the brain that contains these neurons is larger in the left than right hemisphere. To learn if there were anatomic differences, between left- and right-handers, in the motor cortex of their right and left hemispheres, we performed a study measuring the surface area of the motor cortex in the hand and arm region of right-handed and non–right-handed healthy participants using volumetric magnetic resonance imaging (MRI). Imaging of our right-handed participants did reveal a leftward asymmetry. However, we did not find any asymmetries in our non–right-handers. This morphometric study suggests that volumetric asymmetries of the motor cortex may be related to hand preference (Foundas et al., 1996).

In another study, Katrin et al. (1996), using magnetic resonance morphometry, reported that the depth of the central sulcus is related to handedness. In right-handers, the left central sulcus is deeper than the right, and vice versa in left-handers. This macrostructural asymmetry was complemented by a microstructural asymmetry in the motor cortex (Brodmann's area 4) with left-larger-than-right asymmetry in neuropil volume (i.e., tissue compartment containing dendrites, axons, and synapses). These investigators concluded that these asymmetries suggest that hand preference is associated with increased connectivity as demonstrated by an increased neuropil compartment in the left hemisphere's motor cortex and an increased intrasulcal surface of the precentral gyrus in the dominant hemisphere.

Lawrence and Kuypers (1968) had rhesus monkeys retrieve food from large and small holes. When reaching into the large holes, the monkey could get their entire hand into the hole, and in the small holes, these moneys could only get their forefinger and thumb into the hole and use a pincer (precise) grasp to retrieve the food. After their corticospinal tract was cut in the bottom of their brain stem, these monkeys could not retrieve small pieces of food from the small holes using the pincer grasp. However, they were able to use a palmer grasp, where all the fingers are simultaneously flexed against the palm, in order to get some food out of the large holes. Very young children do not have fully developed corticospinal systems and before this system becomes functional, they also use a palmer grasp to lift items.

In front of the motor cortex there is a cortical area called the premotor cortex (Figure 1.4). This is the area that selectively activates the neurons in the motor cortex. Studies have suggested that the premotor cortex is also important for pro-gramming deft movements (Fogassi et al., 2001; Nirkko et al., 2001). However, its role in asymmetries of hand-finger deftness, and handedness, remains unclear.

A greater number of upper motor neurons in the left than right hemisphere would produce a higher ratio of upper to lower motor neurons, which may allow for greater precision of movements. It is also possible that in right-handers the motor cortex in the left hemisphere could be more selectively activated than the motor cortex in the right hemisphere and this selectivity could be mediated by the premotor cortex.

Spatial-Temporal Programing of Skilled Purposeful Movements

There is another brain asymmetry that might account for hand preference. In order to perform skilled movements, when working with tools and objects, a person has to know how to correctly posture their hand and arm to correctly hold the tool and to correctly interact with the object with which they want to move and also know the joints that must be moved, the relative timing of these joint movements, and the speed of these movements.

In addition to describing limb-kinetic apraxia, Hugo Liepmann (1920) described another disorder he called ideomotor apraxia. When patients with ideomotor apraxia attempted to make skilled movements, they made several types of spatial errors, including postural errors and spatial movement errors. The postural errors are the incorrect placement of the arm, hand, and fingers at their initial position. The movement errors are caused by moving the incorrect joint or joints as well as incorrectly timing the interactions between joint movements. For example, when asked to show how to use a screwdriver to put a screw into a wall, a patient with ideomotor apraxia might rotate their hand at their wrist rather than rotate the forearm at the elbow. If asked to show how they would slice a loaf of bread with a knife, instead of making the movements that would move the knife forward and backward, they may make chopping movements. To make slicing movements, a person needs to move their forearm at the elbow forward while they are also making forward movements at their shoulder and then perform the opposite movement, but with each movement, the elbow is less flexed so that the knife moves downward. Patients with ideomotor apraxia may just move their arm at the elbow and this will cause them to make chopping movements. In addition, they might fail to move their hand or tool in the correct direction, and therefore when slicing bread, they make their slices of bread uneven (Rothi et al., 1988; Poizner et al., 1990). Patients with ideomotor apraxia can also make movement speed errors (Poizner et al., 1990).

There are several areas of the brain when damaged can cause ideomotor apraxia. One of the areas is in the inferior parietal lobes (Figure 1.8). This area receives input from multiple sensory systems, including the visual networks and the somesthetic networks (touch and movement perception). Using this information, the inferior parietal lobe can develop memories (representations) of how learned skilled movements look like and how they feel. Studies of patients with injury to this area of the brain reveal that these patients cannot correctly program skilled movements, and in the absence of these representations, they cannot recognize if someone else is making correct or incorrect skilled movements (Heilman & Rothi, 2012).

In patients who are right-handed it is the left parietal lobe that appears to store these visuospatial-kinesthetic movement representations (memories of what limb movements feel like and look like) and damage to the left inferior parietal lobe impairs these memories or knowledge of what skilled movement looks like and feels like for both the left and right arms and hands.

Studies using functional imaging have also revealed that the inferior parietal lobe becomes activated when healthy people are performing these skilled movements, and it is primarily the supramarginal gyrus that stores these spatial and temporal representations. These representations are sensory representations, and in order to correctly perform these skilled movements, this information has to be sent to the

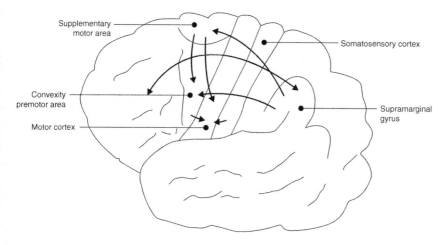

FIGURE 1.8 Connectivity of the Premotor Cortex, the Supplementary Cortex, with the Motor Cortex

There are two areas that are part of the premotor network. One is directly in front of the motor cortex, called the convexity premotor. Another area of the premotor cortex is also in front of the motor cortex, but it is more dorsal (high up) and is called the supplementary motor cortex. This figure shows the major input and output connections with the premotor cortex. The premotor cortex has a strong connection with the motor cortex. The premotor cortex selectively activates the motor neurons in the motor cortex. The premotor cortex also receives information from the inferior parietal lobe about the movements needed to perform a motor task. The more lateral portions of the premotor cortex appear to be, in part, dependent on sensory input and those that are superior and more medial appear to be important in programming of movements that are self-initiated.

premotor areas in the frontal lobes. The brain has several large cables that connect different areas of the brain. One of these, called the superior longitudinal fasciculus, connects the inferior parietal lobe with the premotor cortex and supplementary motor area (Figure 1.9) and it is these areas that convert these visual-kinesthetic movement representations into motor programs. Injury to these areas also causes ideomotor apraxia. However, unlike the patients with a left parietal lesion, these patients can recognize correctly from incorrectly performed learned skilled actions. The supplementary and premotor cortex connect with the primary motor cortex, and it is the selective activation of the motor cortex that allows us to perform learned skilled movements (Figure 1.8).

In right-handed people, it is left hemisphere lesions of this network that causes ideomotor apraxia. Although perhaps not as well done as when using their right hand, right-handed people can perform learned skilled movement with their left hand. When the corpus callosum is injured and the right hemisphere is disconnected from the left, patients can exhibit an ideomotor apraxia of just their left arm and hand (Watson & Heilman, 1983)

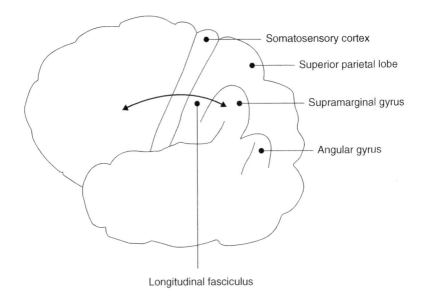

Somatosensory cortex

Superior parietal lobe

Supramarginal gyrus

Angular gyrus

Longitudinal fasciculus

FIGURE 1.9 The Inferior Parietal Lobe

The inferior parietal lobe has two major areas. One is the supramarginal gyrus, which surrounds the ascending limb of the Sylvian fissure. The other is the angular gyrus, which surrounds the posterior end of the superior temporal sulcus. Both of these areas of the inferior parietal lobe get input from visual, auditory, and somesthetic sensory association areas. Injury to the left angular gyrus can cause a disorder called Gerstmann's syndrome. Patients with this disorder have trouble knowing their right from left side (right–left confusion); knowing the names of their fingers (finger agnosia); performing arithmetic, such as addition, subtraction, multiplication, and division; and a loss of the ability to write. Injury to the left supramarginal gyrus causes ideomotor apraxia. The left supramarginal gyrus stores information about the spatial and temporal components of meaningful movements and sends this information to the premotor cortex by a large cable of axons called the superior longitudinal fasciculus. Injury to this network causes a loss of the ability to perform learned skilled movements, called ideomotor apraxia.

Hugo Liepmann (1920) thought that it was the left hemispheric location of this praxis network that was responsible for right-handedness, Norman Geschwind and Edith Kaplan (1962) described a man who developed a brain tumor and while this tumor was being removed by the surgeons, they clamped a bleeding artery that supplies blood to the corpus callosum and this patient developed an infarction of the corpus callosum. After this patient recovered from surgery, when tested, this patient's right arm and hand's actions when performing skilled movements to command, imitation, and with actual objects were entirely normal. However, he could not carry out skilled movements to verbal command with his left hand. However, he could imitate skilled movements and normally use tools with his left hand. This dissociation between verbal command and imitation suggests that this patient's comprehension of verbal commands was mediated by his left hemisphere, and with the callosal injury, this information could not get from the left hemisphere to the right hemisphere. However, this right-handed man's right hemisphere did appear to be able to program skilled movement when they were not dependent on comprehending speech. This observation did not appear to support Liepmann's handedness hypothesis since if the knowledge of how to perform skilled movement is stored in the left hemisphere of right-handed people, a callosal disconnection should have also impaired this man's ability to perform learned skilled movement to repetition and to correctly use tools and implements.

Bob Watson and I (1983) did report a right-handed woman who had a brain hemorrhage, which occurred between her right and left hemispheres. This blood caused the blood vessels that feed the corpus callous with blood to go into spasm, deprive the corpus callosum of oxygen, and cause an infarction injury. Unlike the patient reported by Norman Geschwind and Edith Kaplan, this lovely woman was unable to perform skill movements with her left hand and arm to verbal instructions, imitation, or use tools even when given actual tools. Subsequently, there have been many other similar reports suggesting that in many people the left hemisphere does indeed store the programs needed for making skilled movements with the left hand.

Berthier, Starkstein, and Leiguarda (1987) reported a right-handed man who developed an ideomotor apraxia from a right hemisphere lesion and Króliczak, Piper, and Frey (2016), using functional imaging, found the some left-handed people activated their left inferior parietal lobe when performing skilled movements. These studies suggest that the lateralization of praxis representations and praxis pro-graming does not fully account for handedness. However, it remains possible that hand preference is multifactorial and the lateralization of praxis programs is a factor in hand preference.

Motor Learning

Hugh Liepmann (1908) suggested another factor he thought might be an important factor in the determination of handedness—motor learning. Motor learning is much different from other forms of learning. For example, the famous patient HM who had both temporal lobes removed, and developed a dramatic impairment in episodic memory (anterograde amnesia), so that he could not recall any activities he performed or people with whom he met the prior day, had his motor learning assessed by Susan Corkin (1968). Corkin had HM train with a rotatory pursuit apparatus. When performing this task, HM had to attempt to keep the tip of a metal wand on a metal disk that was rotating, like a record on an old phonograph. Each day, when he was brought into the research laboratory, he did not recall using this apparatus and the instructions for using this apparatus had to be repeated each day. He also did not recall some of the people who were performing this testing. However, when he repeatedly used this rotatory pursuit apparatus, his motor skills improved. The results revealed that unlike episodic memory, where encoding is

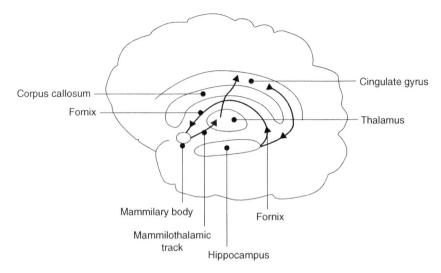

Corpus callosum

Fornix

Cingulate gyrus

Thalamus

Mammilary body

Fornix

Mammilothalamic
track

Hippocampus

FIGURE 1.10 The Papez Circuit

The Papez circuit that includes the hippocampus, the fornix, the mammillary body, the mammillothalamic tract, the thalamus, the cingulate, and retrosplenial cortex was originally thought to be important in emotions. However, after the patient HM had his hippocampi removed to help control his seizure, he developed a severe loss of his episodic memory. Subsequently, clinicians became aware that injury to many other parts of this circuit can also impair episodic memory.

mediated by the hippocampi and other portions of the Papez circuit (Figure 1.10), learning of a motor skill relies on a different network.

We (Taylor & Heilman, 1980) requested that healthy right-handed participants attempt to learn a new sequential key pressing motor skill. They attempted to learn one pattern with their right and a different pattern with their left hand, but both these patterns were of equal difficulty. We found that the right hand learned this skilled series of movements better than did the left hand. We also examined the relationship between hand dominance and transfer of skill to the opposite hand. We attempted to learn if these healthy participants learned a skill with one hand (left or right) and the other hand was tested, would the left-hand benefit more from the right hand learning this skill or vice versa. We found that when these right-handed participants were trained in a new motor skill with their right hand or their left hand and then the opposite hand was tested, there was a greater transfer from left hand learning to the right-hand performance than vice versa. This result suggests that when learning a new skill with the left hand, this motor skill is being stored more by the ipsilateral (left) hemisphere than vice versa. This finding provides even further support for Liepmann's hypothesis that motor learning may be a factor in determining handedness.

On the basis of Liepmann's (1920) hypothesis that the left hemisphere of right-handed people contains the representations of learned skilled actions and that ideomotor apraxia can be caused by a destruction of these representations (memories), patients with ideomotor apraxia from left hemisphere lesions should not only show apraxic performance errors but also be impaired in learning new motor skills. To test this hypothesis, we studied a group of right-handed patients with left hemisphere strokes who had or did not have an ideomotor apraxia to see if they could learn a new motor skill (Heilman, Schwartz & Geschwind, 1975). We used a rotary pursuit to test motor learning. All the participants were instructed to use their left (non-paretic) hand. The performance of the stroke patients who were without an ideomotor apraxia significantly improved with repeated trials. However, the patients with ideomotor apraxia did not reveal any significant improvement with repeated trials. The results of this study provided evidence that the left hemisphere network important in programming learned skilled movements is also important for learning new motor skills, and hand preference might also be related to asymmetries of learning (procedural memories).

Alternative Actions

Most purposeful actions require preparation. However, often after preparation, there is a need to inhibit this preparation and perform an alternative action. For example, the quarterback during a football game prepares to throw the ball to a wide receiver but notices that this receiver just tripped. He also sees that the defensive guard from the opposing team is coming in to tackle him. Therefore, he rapidly puts the ball against his chest and starts to run. We designed an experiment to learn if there are hemispheric asymmetries in the ability to withhold a planned action and instead perform an alternative action (Shenal, Hinze & Heilman, 2012). (Figures 1.11–1.13). We provided healthy participants with cues (warning stimuli), both valid and invalid, that indicated which hand (right versus left) would be most likely to be called to respond. The greatest majority of these cues (80%) were valid-correct. Following these cues, a second stimulus (imperative stimulus) was presented, which instructed these participants to initiate a movement with a specific hand. These stimuli were presented to either the right or left visual fields of right-handed participants. The delay in initiating a response after a miscue is the time taken to inhibit the brain's motor systems in one hemisphere that was incorrectly activated, as well as to activate the motor systems of the opposite hemisphere, which might have been interhemispherically inhibited by this miscue. We found that the miscues presented in left hemispace (to the right hemisphere) cost more time than those presented in right hemispace (to the left hemisphere). These results suggest that activation of the preparatory motor systems controlled by the right hemisphere may take longer to reverse than those controlled by the left hemisphere and this asymmetry may provide another advantage that righted people have when using their right hand.

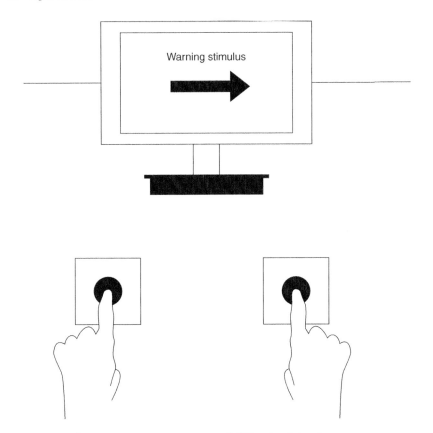

FIGURE 1.11 The Motor Preparation Test—Valid Warning Stimulus

The participant being tested sits in front of a screen. The viewer is asked to view the screen. On most trials the screen will show a warning stimulus, which be a short arrow, that points the left or to the right. These warning stimuli indicate which hand (right versus left) will be most likely to be called on to respond, as shown on a screen after the warning stimulus goes off.

Right-Hander's Use of Their Left Hand

In an earlier section, we discussed how in right handers, it is their right hand and fingers that have ability to make more precise, independent but coordinated finger movements than does their left hand and fingers. When you watch right-handed people play stringed instruments, such as a violin, often use their left hand rather their right hand to play the notes. With a violin, the right hand is used to move the bow back and forth, but when playing the guitar, the right hand is used to strum the strings of the guitar.

In order to produce these notes with their left hand, these musicians must often make rapid, independent, and precise finger movements. Since, as discussed earlier,

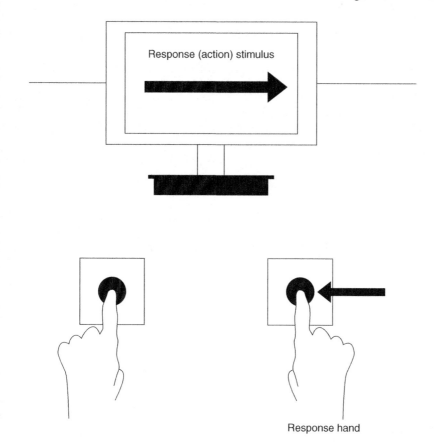

FIGURE 1.12 Response to Imperative Stimulus Following Valid Warning Stimulus

The imperative (action-go) stimulus is a longer arrow that indicates the hand that should press the button. The warning stimulus is valid (correct) on 80% of the trials and incorrect (invalid) on 20% of the trials.

right-handers normally have greater finger dexterity-deftness with their right than their left hand, why would right-handed musicians use their left hand to play notes?

The answer to this question is not entirely known. However, Brenda Milner (1962) studied patients who had undergone temporal lobectomy for control of their epileptic seizures. To test how removal of their left or right temporal lobe might have altered their musical abilities, Milner et al. tested these patients with a test called the Seashore Tests of Musical Ability. This test was devised by the American psychologist Carl Seashore (1866–1949) and he discussed this test in his book *The Psychology of Musical Talent* (1919). This test measures six musical aptitudes including discrimination of pitch, loudness, rhythm, time, timbre, and tonal memory (melody). Brenda Milner's study reported that right temporal lobectomy led to a

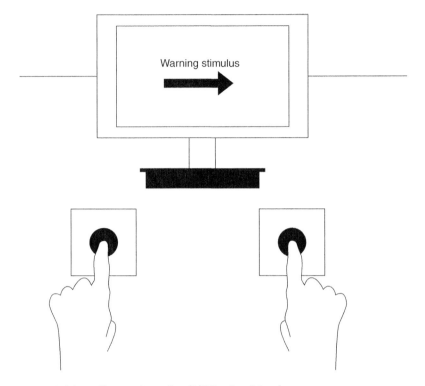

FIGURE 1.13 Motor Preparation—Invalid Warning Stimulus

The figure shows an invalid warning stimulus (20% of trails). Following these invalid cues, a second stimulus is presented (imperative stimulus), indicating that the hand that was not prepared for action should be the hand that should be used to press the response key. The order in which these valid versus invalid stimuli and no warning stimuli are presented and that hand required to press the response key are all randomized.

decline in these patient's scores on the tonal memory and timbre tests. Left temporal lobectomy impaired rhythm.

Each hemisphere has more direct access to the motor systems in the same hemisphere. Thus, the right hemisphere, which mediates melody, has stronger connections with the motor cortex of the right hemisphere which controls the left hand. This might be the reason why when right-handers play string instruments, they use their left hand to play melody. In addition, the left hemisphere appears to be more important in timing and rhythm, and when playing instruments, such as the guitar, it is often the right hand's movements that are responsible for determining the rhythm.

Another activity where the left hand appears to play a critical role is shooting a rifle or using a bow and arrow. For example, when shooting a rifle, the most

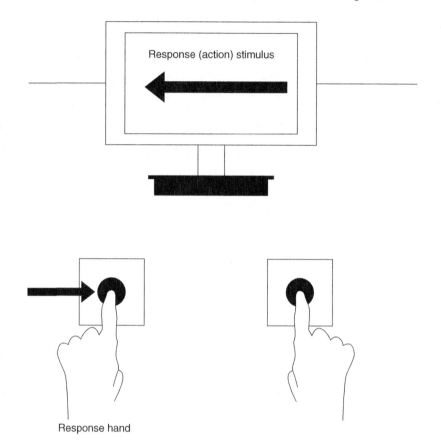

Response (action) stimulus

Response hand

FIGURE 1.13 Cont.

important part is aiming the rifle, and when right-handers shoot a rifle, most will use their left hand to aim the rifle and use a finger of their right hand, such as the index finger, to pull the trigger. Pulling a trigger does not require much skill, but correctly aiming a rifle requires skill. The same can be said of shooting an arrow with a bow. The right hand does pull back the bowstring and then releases the bowstring, but the aiming is again mediated by the left hand. Studies of patients with strokes as well as functional imaging have revealed that the right hemisphere appears to be dominant for visuospatial processing. Since aiming a rifle or a bow and arrow the right hemisphere has better direct access to the left than the right upper extremity, we might use the left arm and hand to aim these implements.

Proximal Versus Distal

There is, however, another reason why the rifle and bow might be held with the left arm extended and the right arm more flexed as well as why on many stringed instruments notes are played with the left hand while the right strums or holds the bow.

When I was a boy growing up in Brooklyn, I had an older brother, Fred. He was a wonderful brother, but like many older brothers, he taught me to fight (box). I also learned that the New York City Police Department had what was called the Police Athletic League (PAL) and one of the sports they sponsored was boxing. When I took some boxing lessons at the PAL, I was told that since I was right-handed, when I box my right arm and hand should be held close to my body and my left arm should also be flexed at my elbow but not as close to my body as my right hand. When I asked why, I was told that with my left hand I should perform "jabs." A jab is a type of punch where the lead fist (e.g., my left hand would be about eight inches in front of my face) is moved straight ahead at the opponent, most often to their head. When hitting the opponent, the left arm is often fully extended, and the right-handed boxer's body should be turned so the left side of their body is facing their opponent. My instructor told me that my right arm and fist were to be held closer to the body with my right fist being held just under the chin. The right arm and hand can be used to block the opponent's punches and when there is opening, the right arm can be used to strongly punch the opponent. Whereas the left arm primarily performs jabs, the right arm often performs three other types of punches, including the uppercut, when the fist is brought upward, the hook when the fist is brought around in a semicircle, and the straight-cross, when the fist is brought straight ahead. The reason for the left side of my body being held closer to the opponent was that it not only allows me to stand further away from my opponent when I was using my left-handed jabs, but when I decide to punch with my right hand, not only did I move my hand to my opponents head or body, but I would also be able to turn my body in a counterclockwise direction and this would even give greater force to my right-handed punches, and these types of punches could knock my opponent out (unconscious).

When I boxed I did use this posture, with my right hand being close to my chin and chest and my left arm held in front of my face, because when I tried the reverse stance, that left-handed boxer would use, it felt terribly unnatural. Thus, in addition, firing rifles, shooting arrows, and playing stringed instruments, the right hand likes to be closer to the body than does the left hand. Perhaps the reason we hold rifles, bows, and violin like we do has little to do with hemispheric specialization for visuospatial processing or knowledge of melodies, but rather because the right hand likes to be close to our body. Support for the right-hand-likes-to-be-closer hypothesis comes from viewing other activities, such as sweeping with a broom, when the right hand is held closer to the body than the left hand.

I wish I knew a means of learning why right-handed people like to keep their right hand closer to the body. Is it related to hemispheric specialization for the specific activities? Are there differences in the left versus right motor cortex such that in the left hemisphere there is a greater proportion of motor neurons that activate muscles that perform flexion than extension activities of the arm? I cannot answer these questions and think that further research is needed.

Handedness and Allocation of Spatial Attention

As discussed earlier, Paul Broca suggested that hemispheric laterality of language was a critical factor in hand preference. Liepmann (1908), however, proposed that handedness reflects the greater capacity of one hemisphere to learn, program, and execute skilled movements. Although hemispheric asymmetries of language processing and motor control are important factors in determining the basis for hand preference, handedness may also be influenced by other factors.

When right-handed people have a stroke of their right parietal lobe, they often reveal a disorder called unilateral spatial neglect. As a medical student, one of the experiences that led me to become interested in neurology was seeing a man with unilateral spatial neglect. Patients with disorder appear to be unaware of objects on the left side of their body. For example, if they are presented with a sheet of paper with lines randomly distributed over this sheet of paper and asked to cross out all the lines that they see on the paper, they typically cross out the lines on the side of the page that is on their right side but fail to cross out the lines on their left side. Similarly, when asked to copy or draw a picture they often draw only the right side (Figure 1.14). Some patients with this disorder will also be unaware of someone speaking them who is on their left side. They also may have personal neglect and are unaware of being touched on their left side. The patient I saw in medical school was even unaware of that his left hand and arm even belonged to him.

This disorder, unilateral neglect, is not caused by a loss of sensory input. However, our brain receives more sensory inputs than it can possible fully processes. Therefore, our brain needs to select the information that is most important to us. For example, now when you are reading this material, you may be unaware of the sensory information coming from your left foot. However, when you read this, you will allocate your attention to your foot and feel these sensations. Studies of patients with unilateral neglect have revealed that their unawareness is not caused by a sensory defect but inattention to stimuli presented on their left side.

To learn why this disorder is most commonly caused by right than left hemisphere injury, we performed a study of right-handed healthy adults. We attached electrodes to their head and recorded an encephalogram (EEG) from the area of the skull over the parietal lobes of both their right and left hemispheres (Heilman & Van Den Abell, 1979). When recording an EEG from a healthy relaxed person, they reveal electrical waves and these waves normally have a frequency of about 8–12 waves per second. This is called an alpha rhythm. However, if the portion of the brain under the electrode becomes aroused-activated, this alpha activity is no longer present, and the waves speed up, have a lower amplitude, and may be even more difficult to see. This phenomenon is called desynchronization. We found that when stimuli were presented in left hemispace, the right parietal lobe revealed evidence

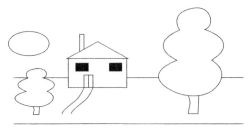

Picture shown to patient and patient asked to copy

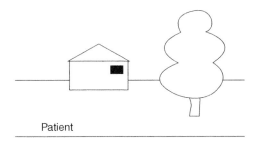

Patient

FIGURE 1.14 Types of Drawings Performed by Patients with Unilateral Spatial Neglect Show a Right Hemisphere Injury

When patients with unilateral spatial neglect, from diseases like stroke, are asked to copy a drawing, such as a scene, they will often just draw the right half of the picture, as displayed in the lower part of the picture. Sometimes this failure to draw the left half of the scene is because they are not attentive or aware of the left side of the picture they have been asked to copy. However, when many of these patients are not asked to copy a picture, but rather to spontaneously draw a picture such as a daisy, these patients will still draw one half of a daisy, suggesting that perhaps they have a failure to perform actions in one half of space. While there are patients who with unilateral neglect do have a failure to act in the space opposite their brain injury, there are even others who, when asked to describe a scene from their memory, will only recall the items on the right side of this scene, suggesting that inattention-spatial neglect can also be for imagery-spatial memory.

of activation (desynchronization) more did the left parietal lobe. In contrast, when we gave these healthy participants stimuli on the right side, both the left and right parietal lobes revealed activation.

When an area of the brain increases in activity, there is an increase of blood flow to this area and functional imaging is a means of examining brain activity by measuring changes in blood flow. Using functional imaging, Pardo et al. (1991) also found a similar functional asymmetry, such that the right hemisphere activated to both left and right spatial stimuli, but the left hemisphere primarily activated to right-sided stimuli. Therefore, the reason why patients with a left parietal lesion remain aware of stimuli on their right side is because their right parietal lobe can allocate attention to the right side.

Since both the right and left hemispheres can allocate attention to the right half of personal space, and the right hemisphere can only allocate attention to left half of space, when interacting with objects in the environment the left hemisphere, which controls the right hand, is more likely to be aware of these stimuli, to be able to process these stimuli, and to be more ready to interact with them than would be the left hand, which would primarily be activated by stimuli just in left hemispace (Figures 1.15–1.17).

We (Verfaellie & Heilman, 1990) tested the hypothesis that these hemispheric attentional asymmetries may contribute to hand preference. We had right-handed participants performed a reaction time task where they were given preliminary information (cues) about where a target stimulus would likely occur (selective spatial attention) or which hand to use for responding (selective action-intention). We found that these processes influence each other such that right hand preparation induced more rapid responses to both right- and left-sided imperative visual stimuli than preparation with the left hand. In addition, warning stimuli presented in right hemispace prepared both hands for action better than stimuli presented in left hemispace. These hemispheric attentional asymmetries therefore appear to contribute to hand preference.

It was also mentioned that when performing certain activities, the right hand is held closer to the body than is the left hand. When something gets our visual attention, we move our eyes so that we can better see that object. When we are using our arms and hands to work with objects, some objects may be close to the body and other objects further from the body. Another possible reason for holding our right hand closer to our body than our left hand might be related to how we specially allocate our attention. One means, by which we test the horizontal spatial allocation of attention, is by having participants perform line bisection tests. We draw a line on a piece of paper and ask the person we are testing to mark the middle of the line ("bisect the line"). If more attention is allocated to a certain portion of an object, that object appears to be larger than an object that is less attended. Patients with lesions of their brain have a disorder called neglect, which we discussed earlier, where they are inattentive to contralateral part of space. Thus, when performing the line bisection test, these patients will often deviate their attempted bisections to the right of center. Even healthy people can have alterations of their estimates of length or magnitude with different activities. For example, if you are trying to go to dinner at someone's house and you have never been to their house before this trip, and were not familiar with this house's location, after you found the house and had dinner and drove back to your house, on these same roads, the trip going would appear to be much longer than that returning. Why? Since when driving to this house was unfamiliar and we normally attend to novel items more than familiar items, driving to the house seems much longer than returning, even though you drove at the same speed in both directions.

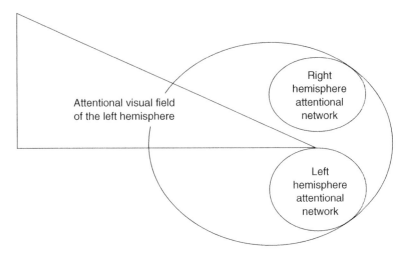

FIGURE 1.15 Standing on the Right Side

Each hemisphere attends to the space that is on the opposite side of her or his body. Therefore, when some person or some event is being viewed, the left hemisphere is more likely to be involved in processing this stimulus if it is on the right side of the viewer's eye, head, and body and the right hemisphere is more likely to attend to stimuli on the left side of space. However, as illustrated in this figure, the left hemisphere primarily attends to the right side of space.

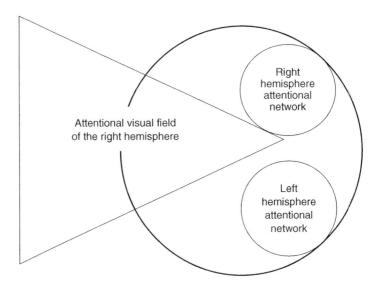

FIGURE 1.16 Standing on the Right or Left

In contrast to the left hemisphere, the right hemisphere can attend to both right and left hemispace; therefore stimuli on the right side of the head and body are attended to by both hemispheres, but stimuli on the left are attended primarily by the right hemisphere.

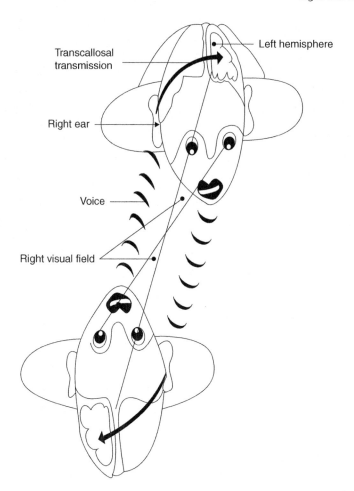

FIGURE 1.17 Standing on Right and Facing Each Other

When a person stands on the right side of another person and these two people are facing each other, their location would activate each of their left hemispheres (as shown in the figure) and this location may be likely to induce a positive mood.

Therefore, when performing the line bisection test, a person deviates to the portion of the line to which they are attending. Szpak, Thomas, and Nicholls (2016) wanted to learn if the right and left hemispheres allocated near versus far spatial attention differently. They tested healthy undergraduate students by having them bisect lines that were perpendicular to their body and these lines were place to the left and to the right of their body's midline. They found that the bisections of the lines on the right were closer to the participant than the lines to the left, suggesting that the left hemisphere pays attention to items that are closer to the body. When interacting with other people, we are usually pretty close and therefore another reason we might like them to be on our right side.

Genetics of Handedness

Although some of the brain mechanisms that may account for handedness have been discussed, it remains unclear what determines handedness. Although many studies have proposed that handedness is determined by genetics, and have provided evidence to support this hypothesis, the genetics of handedness remains unclear. Support for the hypothesis that genetics do play a role in determining handedness comes from the observation that there is a relationship between the handedness of parents and their children but little evidence that with adoption there is a relationship. Laland (2008) estimated that when both parents are right-handed, a child has only an eight percent chance of being left-handed. If one parent is left handed, a child has a 22% chance of being left-handed and if both parents are left-handed, that child has a 36% chance of being left-handed. Further evidence comes from the observation that identical twins are much more likely to have the same hand preference than twins that are not identical (Sicotte et al., 1999). Annett (1998) proposed that there was one gene, called the right shift gene, that determined handedness and laterality of language. If a person has this gene, they are right-handed and left hemisphere dominance for language, but without this gene, the laterality of handedness and language is up to chance. No such gene has been found and McManus et al. (2013) thought that a multiple locus model would better explain handedness than a single locus model, as posited by Annett (1998).

Our findings suggest that handedness is highly polygenic. Our discussion of the many factors that can influence the selection of a hand used for different tasks appears to be most consistent with this multiple locus model, and Gabriel Cuellar-Partida et al. (2021) found 48 genetic variants that are associated with handedness.

Direction of Writing

Before reading this section, please take a writing pad and pencil or pen. Put the writing pad on your forehead, so that the paper is facing away from you and write a word (e.g., "key") on this paper. After you do this, take the paper down, but do not look at what you have written…until later.

In all European languages, when people write and read they start on the left side of the page and move rightward. The reason why in these countries and in these languages people write and read from left to right is not entirely known.

One of the several theories of why in most languages right-handed people write from left to right is the "smear theory." Currently, with the use of ballpoint pens there is a reduced chance of smearing ink, but when almost all writing was done with a fountain pen, if you held the pen in your right hand and wrote from right to left, there would be a greater chance that you would smear the ink before it dried with the lateral part of the hand. Many left-handed people hook their hand when writing, so instead of their index finger and thumb pointing upward while writing, these left-handed people who hook have their wrist bent so that the index finger and thumb are pointing down. One of the theories about why some left-handed people hook is because they are trying to avoid smearing the ink, but there are other theories of why these left-handed people hook their hand when writing.

I learned that when I speak about the shape of the hand when some left-handers write, I need to be careful about calling these people "hookers." Once when I was about to give a lecture at another university, as a visiting professor, I noticed that one of the young women in the audience was writing with her left hand in this curved posture, I said to her, "It looks like you are a hooker." Several people who also came to hear my lecture stood and appeared to be angry about my comment. However, fortunately, this woman stood up and said, "Calm down! All Dr. Heilman means is that when I write with my left hand I bend my wrist and my finger point downward. Some psychologists call this hooking."

It appears that during the Civil War, General Hooker had women prostitutes for his soldiers and these women were called, "Hookers." However, about 90% of the world population is right-handed and most people who are right-handed have language mediated by their left hemisphere. In general, each hemisphere processes information from the opposite side of space, such that the left occipital lobe of the brain processes visual information from the right half of space and vice versa. While sounds coming into each ear are processed by both hemispheres, the right ear projects more strongly to the left hemisphere and the right ear to the left hemisphere. Finally, when you touch something with your right hand, this information is sent primarily to the left hemisphere and information from you left hand is sent to your right hemisphere. It is well known that each hemisphere also controls the opposite side of the body, such that the left hemisphere controls the right hand, arm, and leg and the right hemisphere controls the left arm, hand, and leg. What is not as well known is that each hemisphere primarily controls movements that occur in the opposite direction. For example, if you spontaneously look to the right side (make a saccadic movement), the movement is initiated by the left hemisphere, and if you spontaneously look to the left, it is the right frontal lobe that initiates this movement. In the hospital when we see a patient with a large hemispheric stroke, their eyes will often be deviated toward to side of the stroke.

Please stop reading here, and take a piece of blank paper and pen. Now draw a horizontal line. A line that is parallel to your chest.

Although not as well known, when making right or leftward movements with each hand and arm, the hemisphere that controls that arm prefers to make what are called abductive movements. These are movements that start at the opposite side of the body, as the side of the arm and hand holding the pen, and move toward the same side as that arm.

Did you, like many people, start on the left side of the page and move your hand with the pen from left to right? If you did, you are probably right-handed. If you moved from the right side of the page to the left, you are probably left-handed.

In most right- and left-handed people, the right arm prefers to move from left to right and the left arm from right to left.

In addition, studies of patients who had hemispheric strokes suggest that each hemisphere appears to be important in programming many of the movements of the arm and hand on opposite side such that the left hemisphere's motor cortex controls the right arm and hand, and the left hand and arm are controlled by the motor cortex in the right hemisphere. However, in addition to controlling the movements of the contralateral arm and hand, each hemisphere also plays a role in programming movements of the hand on the same side, in the opposite (contralateral direction). For example, although the right arm is primarily controlled by the left hemisphere, when patients have a large right hemispheric stroke, in addition to having a paralysis of their left arm and hand, they may be impaired at moving the right arm from right to the left. Although occasionally, we do see patients who have this problem in the opposite direction, such that with left hemisphere stroke, they have trouble moving their left arm in a rightward direction. This directional loss of movement is much more common with right than left hemisphere strokes. Several decades ago, we demonstrated that in right-handed people, the left hemisphere primarily controls rightward movements of the arm, but the right hemisphere appears to be able to control movements of the arm in both leftward and rightward directions.

In addition, to processing speech and language, the left hemisphere of most right-handed people also contains the critical information needed for writing, including knowledge of the letters that compose words and the knowledge of how to program the movements that are needed to write letters. For example, there are right-handed people who, when they have a stroke on their left hemisphere in the region of their parietal lobe, develop a disorder called apraxia agraphia. These people know how to spell words but cannot make the correct movements to write words. However, if given a typewriter or word processor, they can normally use these machines to write meaningful messages. Thus, when right-handed people are writing, it is left hemisphere that is activated, and with left hemisphere activation, it would be more natural for right-handed people to move from left to right.

On the basis of the horizontal lateral biases related to using the right hand and having language and writing mediated by the left hemisphere, it is not clear why in Hebrew and Arabic writing occurs in the opposite (right to left) direction. To my knowledge, studies of handedness have revealed that there is little or no differences in the percent of right- or left-handedness in Semitic people compared to Europeans. It is possible the founder or founders of these written languages happen to be left-handed, but there is no evidence to support this hypothesis and this hypothesis would certainly be difficult to prove.

Some of the oldest examples of written documents are in stone. In order to write in stone in the ancient time, it is unlikely that they had a drill and thus probably used some form of a hammer and chisel. When right-handers use a hammer and a chisel, they usually hold the hammer in their right hand and the chisel in their left hand. Thus, when engraving a stone with a hammer and chisel, right-handers would have to start on the right side of the stone and move leftward. It is possible that the primary reason for the right-to-left direction of this writing in these languages is that they were written in stone.

For some reasons that are not known to me, Jews have a strong right-sided religious bias. The mezuzah is a piece of parchment in a decorative case and inscribed with the Jewish prayer "Shema Yisrael Adonai Eloheinu Adonai echad!" ("Hear, O Israel, the Lord (is) our God, the Lord is One"). This mezuzah, by Jewish law, is to be affixed on the right side of the doorway. When saying this Shema, Jews are to cover their eyes with their right hand. A scribe who is writing the Torah scrolls and other holy writings must use their right hand. When reading the Torah in the synagogue, the reader uses a pointer and this is made to look like the right hand. When washing hands upon arising or before eating, the right hand is to be washed first. When holding up a cup of wine during services (the kiddush cup), it should be held in the right hand. On certain holidays like the New Year (Rosh Hashanah) during the service a horn (shofar) is blown. The horn is to be blown from the right side of the mouth. When holding a Torah scroll, it should be held on the right side. There are many other actions and rituals that Jews perform that have to be performed with the right hand or on the right side. Perhaps that is why they started writing from the right side.

Now, look at the writing you did when you put the paper on your forehead. Did you, like many people, performing mirror writing? If yes, it was because, as usual, when you are writing you move your arm and hand from your left to right, but because of the manner in which this paper was positioned in respect to your body, you actually wrote from the right side of the paper to the left. As far as we know, Hebrews and Arabs did not start writing on their forehead (joke).

Emotional Communication

In the 1970s, I received a call from a physician in Orlando. He had a woman in the hospital who was comatose, having seizures, and had a fever. He told me that he was not a neurologist and was not sure what was going on. He did not know how to evaluate her and treat her. I told him how to load her with an anti-seizure medication and the antibiotics to give her in case she had a meningitis, encephalitis, or an abscess and then to send her up here.

She arrived in about 2 hours and we evaluated this woman before there was MRI or even CT imaging. However, we did have radioisotope imaging and EEG. When she arrived, we continued her treatments and found on her EEG that she had evidence that the seizures were starting (phase reversals) from her right inferior parietal region (Figure 1.9). On radioisotope imaging, she revealed evidence of a local encephalitis or abscess in this same region. We did not do a spinal tap because we were worried that she might have brain swelling, and taking fluid from the spinal canal might cause her right hemisphere to herniate downward, causing death. In addition, she appeared to be responding to medication, with no further seizures and a reduction of her fever. She also appeared to be becoming more alert. After several days, she was fully alert and her only deficit appeared to be some inattention to sensory stimuli on her left side (unilateral neglect). Despite an intensive evaluation, we never found what caused this brain abscess. Thus, after she completed her antibiotic treatment, she was discharged but asked to remain on the anti-seizure medication and to return to see me in clinic in about a month, but to call us if she had any new symptoms and not drive a car.

When she returned to our clinic, along with her husband, she appeared to be doing well with no seizures but still some evidence of left-sided inattention. I asked her to continue her anti-seizure medication and to return to see me in about 6 months.

When she returned 6 months later, with her husband, she appeared to be still doing well. She and her husband asked about continuing the anti-seizure medication and I suggested that they continue this medication. Then her husband asked me if he could speak to me outside the examining room. I asked him why he could not speak to me with her in the room and he said he would be uncomfortable doing that. His wife said, "It is okay Dr. Heilman if you speak to him outside."

I took her husband into another room, which was empty, and asked him why he wanted to speak with me. He asked me, "If I leave my wife, will she be able to take care of herself?"

I asked him, "Why do you want to leave her?"

He replied, "We no longer have a meaningful relationship."

I said, "What do you mean by a meaningful relationship? She is your wife!"

He told me, "I worked for many years at a tire factory up in Ohio and saved money to open a store on International Drive when I learned that Disney World would be built nearby. The store I opened sold toys and games for children. The store was doing well, but now with this gas shortage, no one is coming down to Florida and I am going bankrupt. Each day, after I closed the empty store and I came home and was feeling very depressed, but she never appears to be concerned. It's like she does not care about me."

I asked him, "Did you tell her about your troubles and feelings?"

"No! But it was written all over my face and my voice and all the people who knew me, heard me talk, or saw my face would ask me what's wrong?"

I remembered reading a study by Brenda Milner who examined patients who had epilepsy that started in their right or left temporal lobe. These patients' seizures could not be controlled by anti-seizure medications, and therefore, they underwent neurosurgery and had their right or left temporal lobe removed. After they recovered from this surgery, she examined their musical abilities and found that the patients who had their left temporal lobe removed were poor at the rhythm portion of the musical test. In contrast, those who had their right temporal lobe removed were poor at discriminating melody and timbre. When a person expresses an emotion while they are speaking, they often use prosody. ("It is not what you said, but how you said it.") In many respects, the expression of emotional prosody is dependent on changes of pitch, amplitude, and timbre. Therefore, I said to her husband, "Your wife has a brain injury. Maybe she has problems understanding your emotional expressions. Let us go back to her room. I want to do some tests."

When we got back to her room, I said to her, "I'm going to say a sentence. Listen to how I say it, and not the words. Then tell me how I feel." Then I said, "I just won the lottery" with a sad voice.

She said, "You are happy. You just won a lot of money."

I told her again, "Listen to how I say the sentence, and tell me how I feel. Listen to my tone of voice to make this decision, not the meaning of the words." This time I thought I would use a sentence that had little emotional implications. I said, "The boy went up a flight of stairs." This time I used an angry prosody and she again said, "Happy." I looked at her husband and he looked absolutely surprised.

There had been some research that has revealed that when patients have damage to the bottom (ventral) portion of their temporal and occipital lobes of their right hemisphere, they could not recognize the faces of people who they know well, a disorder called prosopagnosia. Although this woman had an injury to another part of her right hemisphere, she might also be impaired in recognizing emotional facial expressions. I, therefore, also wanted to test her ability to understand emotional facial expressions, but I had other patients who were waiting and I was running out of time. I explained to her husband that just like she is unable to recognize the emotional prosody of speech, she may also not be able to recognize emotional facial expressions and that these impairments were probably related to the injury that she had of her right hemisphere. I told him that in future when he wants her to know about the emotions he is feeling, it would be best to tell her in words.

Unfortunately, they never returned to my clinic and thus I never learned if my suggestions helped their communication. Hopefully, this did save their marriage. After seeing her, we also decided to perform research to learn if patients with right hemisphere strokes who damaged the same area of the brain that this woman damaged would also be impaired. We did find that right hemisphere damage does indeed cause an impairment in the comprehension of emotional prosody. Subsequently, another neurologist, Elliott Ross, also performed much research about this disorder; he also reported that right hemisphere injury impairs the comprehension of emotional prosody.

Whereas the auditory nerves coming from each ear bring information to both the right and left hemispheres, each ear has stronger connections with the hemisphere on the opposite side. Neuropsychologists developed a method of learning which hemisphere was dominant in processing different types of auditory information by using a process called dichotic listening. They put earphones on healthy participants and simultaneously presented a series of different words to the right and left ears. They asked these participants the word or words they heard. When right-handed participants told the examiner the words they heard, it was most likely to be the one that was presented to their right ear. This is because it is their left hemisphere that comprehends words and since the right ear has stronger connections to the left than right hemisphere, they were more likely to process the words presented to the right ear. However, when these words were spoken with emotional prosody, the participants were more likely to hear the material presented to their left ear. This asymmetry is caused by the right hemisphere being dominant for comprehending prosody.

So, why would it be important to be on G-D's right side or anybody's right side? When listening to people speak, and the person speaking to you is on your right side and facing you, your right ear and this person's right ear would be closer to the person who is speaking than your left ear or this person's left ear. Therefore, you would be less likely to hear "how it was said" than "what was said." Maybe it is more important to hear "what is said than how it is said."

Although I did not test the comprehension of facial expressions of the woman who had the brain abscess in her right parietal lobe, based on the story her husband provided, it appeared she was unable to understand emotional facial expressions and did not know, based on his facial expressions, that he was depressed. Therefore, subsequently we performed several studies to learn if people who had damage to their right (versus left) hemisphere were also impaired at recognizing emotional faces. We tested patients who had strokes of their left hemisphere and those with strokes of their right hemisphere, as well as healthy people. We found that when compared to people with left hemisphere injuries (strokes), and healthy people, the patients with right hemisphere injuries were impaired in comprehending emotional facial expressions. These results suggest that the right hemisphere is also important for perceiving emotional facial expressions.

Since the right hemisphere appears to be important for perceiving emotional faces, if someone is on your right side and both of you were standing side by side, it would be difficult for you to see this person facial expressions. However, if someone was standing on your right side and facing you, then they then would be standing in your right visual field and you want to be in their right visual field. Objects are seen in the right visual field project to the left hemisphere, and this hemisphere, unlike the right hemisphere, is not dominant for recognizing emotional faces.

The right hemisphere has the representations that store the knowledge of emotional facial expressions, and damage to the right hemisphere not only impairs recognition of emotional faces but also may impair the expression of emotional faces. Several studies have supported this hypothesis. In addition, each hemisphere also controls most of the muscles of the opposite side of the face. To learn if healthy people have an asymmetry of emotional facial expression, Sackheim, Gur, and Saucy (1978) took pictures of healthy people during the time they were expressing six emotions. These pictures of faces were cut in half, down the midline of each face, and each half of face was copied mirror-reversed and put together with its mirror image. With this method, these investigators were able to make an entire face made of the two left halves and a full face made of the two right halves. These investigators then asked healthy participants to grade the intensity of the emotions being expressed by these faces. They found that overall the faces made from the left side of the face were more expressive of emotions than the faces made up from the right half. Thus, if someone is on your right side and facing you, the less emotionally expressive side of their face will project to your right hemisphere (Figures 1.15–1.17).

Moods

Kurt Goldstein (1948) noted that many patients with left hemisphere injuries, caused by diseases such as stroke, who have an impairment in speech (aphasia) and right-sided weakness, often appeared to be depressed-sad and anxious. Goldstein called this disorder the "catastrophic reaction." In contrast, Babinski (1914) noted that patients with right hemisphere disease often appeared indifferent or even euphoric. Subsequently, Denny-Brown, Meyer, and Horenstein (1952) also noted that patients with right hemisphere lesions were often inappropriately indifferent, or demonstrated, "Witzelsucht," a German term for inappropriate jocularity, including making puns, or telling inappropriate jokes or stories. This disorder is most commonly seen in patients with right hemispheric frontal lobe damage. Although there has been some debate about this hemispheric injury dichotomy in mood, Gainotti (1972) studied a large population of patients with left or right hemispheric strokes and found that left hemisphere strokes, especially of the frontal lobe, were often associated with depression and anxiety. In contrast, right hemispheric injury was most often associated with indifference. In addition, Gasparrini et al. (1978) administered the Minnesota Multiphasic Personality Inventory (MMPI) to patients with right and left hemisphere lesions. The MMPI has been widely used as an index of underlying emotional experience. Patients with left hemisphere disease showed a marked elevation on the depression scale on this MMPI. In contrast, patients with right hemisphere disease did not show an elevation of the depression scale.

The reason for this hemispheric dichotomy in mood following hemispheric injury is still not entirely understood. Unlike patients who have left hemisphere lesions and are aware of their aphasia and their right-sided weakness, patients with a right hemisphere stroke often have severe left-sided inattention, and this inattention may not only cause unawareness of objects on the left side of their body and head (unilateral special neglect), but these patients are also often unaware of the left side of their body and therefore do not know about their disability. Therefore, Gainotti (1972) thought that the indifference reaction, associated with right hemispheric strokes, was being caused by anosognosia (unawareness of disease) and that the catastrophic reaction with a left hemisphere stroke was a normal response to a serious physical or cognitive deficit.

Seizures or epilepsy is often caused by a type of short circuit in a portion of the brain and can occur in either the right or left hemisphere. This short circuit can then spread to other parts of the brain, and as this seizure spreads, it often becomes generalized. A generalized seizure disorder is most often characterized by an initial tonic phase where the patient's trunk and extremities are straight (extended) and stiff. This tonic phase of the generalized seizure is then followed by the clonic phase, where the patient demonstrates rhythmic contractions of the trunk and limbs. Many patients with generalized seizures also have tongue biting, as well as urinary incontinence. Following this convulsion, the patient has a reduced level of consciousness (post-ictal state), which gradually improves over minutes, hours, or even days. Seizures can cause both immediate and long-term disability. Fortunately, many patients with this disorder can be helped with medications, but some do not respond to medications. In 1950, Penfield and Flanigin reported that removal of the portion of temporal lobe, where these seizures often start, could often help stop or reduce the frequency of these seizures.

Each side of the brain performs different functions, and some of these functions are very important, such as understanding speech and encoding new episodic memories. Therefore, removing these parts of the brain can cause a severe disability. Before the development of modern brain imaging techniques that can help to localize specific brain functions, it was important for the neurologists and neurosurgeons to learn the functions of the hemisphere on which they were planning to perform this surgery.

To learn the functions of the hemisphere that the surgeons were planning to operate on, before surgery, they performed the "Wada test." In this test, the physician injects a barbiturate into one of the carotid arteries that supply most of the blood to one hemisphere. This injection stops the functions of the hemisphere that receives the blood supply from this carotid artery. Before the injection, the patient is asked to raise both arms and when the barbiturate is injected in the carotid artery, on one side of the neck, the arm on the other side of injection falls down. The falling arm provides evidence that this hemisphere has been put to sleep. After the arm falls down, the patient's memory and their ability to speak are tested.

Terzian (1964) as well as Rossi and Rosadini (1967) studied the emotional reactions of patients who were recovering their right and left hemispheric functions after their right and left hemispheric anesthesia. They reported that right carotid injections were associated with a euphoric-manic response and the barbiturate injections into the left carotid artery appeared to produce a depressive-catastrophic reaction. Since the left hemisphere anesthesia only causes a transient aphasia with a temporary hemiparesis, this temporary dysfunction would be unlikely to cause a reactive depression in patients who are undergoing this diagnostic test.

The major connection between the right and left hemispheres is the corpus callosum (Figure 1.5). This connection allows the right and left hemispheres to communicate such that information that is stored and the programs mediated by one hemisphere can be transmitted to the other hemisphere. For example, in right-handed people the left hemisphere mediates speech, reading, and writing. Although right-handed people cannot write as well with their left hand (controlled by the right hemisphere) as they can with their right hand, they are able to write with their left hand. They are able to write with their left hand because the programs and knowledge needed to write can be transferred from the left to the right hemisphere by the corpus callosum. However, each hemisphere mediates different types of functions, and for this hemispheric specialization to occur, there also has to be interhemispheric inhibition (e.g., this is my job, not yours). Thus, when a hemisphere is injured not only is there a loss of the functions mediated by the injured hemisphere but also a loss of interhemispheric inhibition. Since the left hemisphere appears to mediate positive emotions and the right hemisphere negative emotions, with left hemisphere injury there is disinhibition of the right hemisphere and the release of negative emotions such as depression and anxiety. In contrast, with right hemisphere injury, there is a release of left hemisphere-mediated positive emotions.

The reason that the left hemisphere appears to mediate positive emotions and the right negative emotions is not entirely known. In our brain and body, there is a system called the autonomic nervous system. This system helps to control many of our internal organs such as the heart, stomach, and intestines; the respiratory system; and blood vessels. This system also controls our sweating and even the size of our pupils.

The autonomic nervous system has two major divisions: one of these networks is called the sympathetic system and the other the parasympathetic system. A detailed account of these two networks would require an entire book. However, the functions of these two systems are very different. In general, we can classify almost all activities of mammals into two major domains. One is protection, or "fight or flight," and the other is survival, including "feed and breed" as well as "digest and rest." The sympathetic system alters the organs of the body so that it can fight or flight and the parasympathetic system allows us to feed and breed as well as digest and rest. For example, when the sympathetic system becomes active and prepares us to fight or flight, it diverts blood flow away from the gastrointestinal (GI) tract and skin by constricting the blood vessel (vasoconstriction), except the arteries that go to the heart. This vasoconstriction allows more blood to be delivered to the skeletal muscles. In order to fight or flight, the muscles need more oxygen and increase activation of the sympathetic nervous system dilates our lungs breathing tubes, the bronchioles. This oxygen needed by the muscles is carried by the blood, and with activation of the sympathetic nervous system, the heart beats more rapidly and contracts more strongly and this also allows more blood to go to the muscles as well as to the lungs to pick up more oxygen. In addition, to enhancing muscle function, activation of the sympathetic system also allows the pupils to dilate so that more light enters the eyes. Finally, when muscles are working hard, there is much energy being used and burning energy increases heat. The active sympathetic nervous system increases our sweating and sweating with evaporation cools our bodies and helps to prevent overheating.

The parasympathetic nervous system performs almost the opposite actions, including increasing the blood flow to the gastrointestinal tract, which increases digestion, encourages secretion of the salivary gland, needed for eating and is even important for stimulating sexual arousal.

If the right hemisphere is dominant for mediating negative emotions, such as fear and anger, that are associated with fight and flight, because this hemisphere also is dominant for controlling the sympathetic nervous system, then with injury to the right hemisphere there should be a reduction in sympathetic activity. More than four decades ago, we (Heilman, Schwartz & Watson, 1978) studied arousal of patients with lesions of the right hemisphere, who exhibit emotional indifference, aphasic patients with lesions of the left hemisphere, and in non-brain-damaged controls, by stimulating the forearm ipsilateral to the side of the brain lesion while recording skin conduction responses (galvanic skin responses) from the fingers on the same side. The patients with right hemisphere strokes had lower skin conduction responses than did the left hemisphere damaged aphasia patients, or non-brain-damaged controls. In this study, we found that the aphasic patients with left hemispheric stroke had even greater skin conduction responses than did non-brain-damaged controls and the right hemisphere damaged patients. These results suggest that right hemisphere mediates sympathetic activity that is important in hemispheric arousal. This disorder of arousal may be responsible, in part, for the flattened affect. The heightened GSR in aphasic patients, with left hemisphere lesions may reflect disinhibition of the right hemisphere and the sympathetic nervous system, which might be partly responsible for increased emotionality in these patients.

One of the most important areas of the brain for producing emotional feeling and behaviors is a nucleus in the front of the temporal lobe called the amygdala. When left-handed people are performing actions, they are more likely to activate the right than left hemisphere and right-handed people would be more likely to activate their left hemisphere. If, as discussed earlier, the left hemisphere mediates positive emotions-moods and the right negative emotions-moods, such as anxiety and depression, would people who are left-handed might be more likely to be depressed or be anxious because they are more likely to activate their right hemisphere than right-handed people, who are more likely to activate their left hemisphere?

Unfortunately, I was unable to find much research that tested these hypotheses. However, I found two interesting articles. Hicks and Pellegrini (1978) examined the anxiety scores of 23 left-handed and 35 right-handed college students. They found that right-handers were significantly less anxious than the left-handed group. However, these authors were cautious and suggested that conclusions may be premature.

Denny (2009) performed a study where the possible link between handedness and depression was investigated. This study used a large population survey from 12 European countries to measure the association between handedness and depression. Results of this study, using three different measures, revealed that left-handers are significantly more likely to have depressive symptoms than right-handers.

Another word for left-handed is sinistral. I could not fully learn why left-handedness is sinister, but there are several possibilities. This word was first recorded in 1425–75; a late Middle English word that means portending evil, harm, trouble, unfortunate, disastrous, or unfavorable. One of the explanations for referring to the left hand as sinister comes from the Middle Ages, when some people would keep a hidden dagger in their left sleeve and used their traitorous left hand to use this dagger. There are several other reasons why being left-handed might have been considered as sinister. One possibility, as mentioned earlier, is the higher rate of depression and anxiety associated with left-handedness. Unilateral brain injury can happen when infants are in their mother's womb, or during birth. Unilateral hemispheric injury can change a child's handedness. For example, if a child was going to be right-handed and has a left hemisphere injury, there is a high probability that child would be left-handed. Since 90% of babies will be right-handed and 10% left-handed, if the right and the left hemispheres have the same chance of being injured, there is a higher probability for right-handers to be converted to a left-hander than left-handers being converted to a right-hander. Hemispheric damage of infants can cause terrible disabilities. Thus, if a right-handed mother and father have a left-handed child, it may be a sign of hemispheric damage and future troubles with disabilities that can be disastrous…sinister.

Even healthy left-handed children will often have more difficulty in performing many activities than will right-handed children. The left-handed child will often sit at the left end of the table when eating, so that when they are slicing with a knife, they will not be as likely to elbow the right-handed person sitting next to them. In addition, each hand prefers to move toward its own side (abductive movements), but when writing left-handers have to make adductive (left-to-right) movements. In addition, many tools and instruments are made for right-handers and thus left-handers often have to learn to use their right for using several tools.

When a person stands on the right side of another person and these two people are facing each other, their location would activate each of their left hemispheres (Figure 1.17) and this location may be likely to induce a positive mood.

Politics: Left and Right

In politics, the terms "left" and "right" are often used. It appears that terms left and right were first used in France during the French Revolution of 1789. At that time in France, the members of the National Assembly were divided. There were some who supported the king, who were to the right, and those who supported the revolution who were to the left. One of the deputies, the Baron de Gauville, explained: "We began to recognize each other: those who were loyal to religion and the king took up positions to the right of the chair so as to avoid the shouts, oaths, and indecencies that enjoyed free rein in the opposing camp."

Two year later, the National Assembly was replaced in 1791 by a Legislative Assembly. Although there were many new members it appears that spatial positions continued. The "Innovators" sat on the left, the "moderates" in the center, and the conservative "conscientious defenders of the constitution" sat on the right. After Bourbon Restoration (1814–30) in France, when Napoleon I abdicated and the Bourbon monarchs and Louis XVIII became king, the majority of legislators who were ultra-royalists sat on the right and the "independents" sat on the left. In the following decades and even with the establishment of the Third Republic in 1871, which lasted 70 years, this left-right dichotomy persisted.

A similar right-left division also occurred in the United Kingdom and even up to the present time in American politics. Currently, in America, the most liberal politicians, which are usually Democrats, are considered to be on the left and sit to the left. In contrast, those representatives who are more conservative, which are most often Republicans, are considered to be on the right and sit on the right.

I tried to learn why in so many countries conservatives sit to the right of liberals. Every person sees the world through his or her own eyes, and since this book is about the brain and I am a neurologist, I would like to propose an unlikely neurological explanation. There are now several functional imaging methods such as MRI and even using EEG to help learn what parts of the brain are processing incoming stimuli. However, about 50 years ago when psychologists were doing research on brain lateralization of language and speech processing, they used a technique called dichotic listening. Each ear sends auditory information to both hemispheres, but sounds coming into the left ear are primarily sent to the right hemisphere and those coming into the right ear are sent to the left hemisphere. More than 95% of right-handed people process incoming speech information by their left hemisphere and even about 70% of left-handers have left hemisphere dominance for processing incoming speech. When researchers wanted to know if the right or left hemisphere was dominant for processing incoming speech, they would perform a test called dichotic listening. When performing this test, they would place earphones on the left and right ears and at the same time (simultaneously) present words to the left and right ears; however, the words presented to the two ears would be different. When right-handers and most left-handers were asked the words they heard, they reported the words they heard in their right ears. If someone is conservative, likes current conditions, and therefore does not want change, new information will not be of as much value to this person as it will to someone who is more liberal and is looking for new ideas and a change in conditions.

Sometime the politicians sitting on the right may want to hear the politicians on the left, because they might be saying something important. However, after they start listening to the speaker on the left, they might not like what they are hearing and want to withdraw their attention.

Michael Posner developed an attention test that he used to assess the participant's ability to disengage their attention when it was incorrectly spatially allocated. When performing this task, healthy participants were instructed to press a key as rapidly as possible after the onset of an imperative stimulus, such as a green light. If the green light was on the left side, they were to use their left hand to press the key on their left side and if the green light was on their right side, they were to press the right-sided key. There were five warning conditions—valid warning stimuli on the left side, valid warning stimuli on the right side, invalid warning stimuli on the left side, invalid warning stimuli on the right side, and no warning stimuli. On the trials when there were warning stimuli, the warning stimuli were valid in 80% of the trials, and in 20% of the trials, they were invalid.

Investigators have found that valid warning stimuli do shorten the reaction times, when compared to trials where there were no warning stimuli. In contrast, when the invalid stimuli are presented, the reaction times are even slower than when there was no warning stimulus. This result has been explained by the postulate that when an invalid warning stimulus is presented, the participants have to disengage their attention from the incorrect stimulus as well as disengage their motor preparatory network from responding with the incorrect hand and instead attend to the imperative stimulus and initiate an action with the opposite hand. Investigators also found right, left asymmetries of how long it took to disengage from left versus right side stimuli. Results revealed that disengagement from left-sided stimuli were more rapid than disengaging from right-sided stimuli.

Now, in regard to politics, this would mean that those politicians on the right could more easily disengage their attention from those speakers on the left than a listener on the left side could disengage from speaker on the right side. Therefore, overall, if you are more conservative, resistant to change, and you don't want to listen to all those who want to make changes, or after listening for a while, and you want to turn them off and stop listening, you are better off being on the right side.

When I was completing my fellowship at the Harvard Neurological Unit in Boston and getting ready to move to Gainesville, Florida, the Chair, Dr. Norman Geschwind, asked me to come into his office. After I thanked him for helping to train me, he offered me some advice. He told me, "Ken, as a man you have to be careful when you lecture and write papers. You should if at all possible never speak or write about sex–gender differences." I asked him, "Why?" He replied, "As a man no matter what you write or say about women, to many women, this will appear to be biased." I have tried to be careful, but forgive me Dr. Geschwind for writing the following.

The United States Congress has 535 members. There are 126 women, which is about 23.6 % of the members of congress. Of those 126 women, 105 are Democrats and 21 Republicans. There appears to be some difference between the means by which men and women allocate spatial attention.

Patients with a stroke of their right hemisphere appear to be more inattentive to contralateral (left-sided) stimuli than are patients with a left hemisphere stroke inattentive to (right-sided) stimuli. A clinician usually assesses hemispatial attention with several tests, but one of these tests is the line bisection test. In this test, the patients is presented with a long horizontal line (approximately 200–240 millimeters) and asked to place a mark in the middle of this line. When a person is inattentive to one side of space, they will underestimate the size of the line on that side of space and therefore patients with right hemispheric strokes and left hemispatial neglect often underestimate the left side of the line and deviate their attempted bisection to the right of midline.

About 40 years ago Dawn Bowers and I thought, "Well if the right hemisphere is dominant for mediating spatial attention, when healthy right-handed adults attempt to bisect a line, they should also deviate slightly to the left." That is what we found (Bowers & Heilman, 1980) and this finding has been replicated by many others (Jewell & McCourt, 2000). Although not all studies find sex differences, Roig and Cicero (1994) found that when men and women were asked to bisect a set of horizontal lines with each hand "men's had a significantly greater deviation to the left (pseudoneglect) than women's deviation."

Now, if men are more likely to attend to the left, why then would there be in congress many more men than women who are members of the Republican Party?

Direction of Action

Before you read the remainder of this section, I would like you to perform a little self-experiment. Usually, at universities before we can perform an experiment, we have to get approval from a committee called the IRB (institutional review board). This IRB reviews the methods proposed for a research project to ensure that they are ethical and will not be harmful to the participants. The purpose of the IRB is to assure that appropriate steps are taken to protect the rights and welfare of humans participating in a research study. Although the following has not been approved by the IRB, it is low risk, and you may find it of interest. To perform this study please get a piece of paper and pencil or pen. Put the paper in front of you on a table. Now with your right hand draw a horizontal line. Then draw an arrow in the direction (rightward versus leftward) that you drew this line.

On a separate piece of paper, draw using stick figures of a girl hitting a boy with a club. Your performance on this task and the meaning of this is discussed below.

All animals, including humans, perform actions and these actions most often alter the objects, people (others and ourselves), as well as plants and animals who are the recipient of these actions. When using language (speaking and writing) to describe this relationship, the performer (doer) of the action is called the "agent" and the recipient of the action is called the "patient." Typically, when speaking and writing people use active declarative sentences (e.g., "The boy hit the girl"). In these sentences, the agent (the boy) is most often spoken or written, before the patient (the girl). With passive sentences (e.g., "the girl was hit by the boy'), the patient is spoken before the agent; however, active sentences are used much more often than passive sentences.

People may express about thematic roles using visuospatial relationships. For example, when drawing they may include in this process both the relative spatial position of the agent (the person performing the action) and the patient (the person receiving the action), as well as the direction of the action between the agent and patient. Chatterjee, Maher & Heilman (1995) had people perform a task similar to that we asked you to do. We asked healthy participants to draw stick figures depicting the thematic roles of agent and patient. We examined these figures and found a systematic spatial bias in locating the agent to the left of where they located patients and most actions went in a rightward direction. The results suggest that the thematic roles of agent and patient are spatially represented in our brain such that we see the patient toward the right of the agent. Is this why, as we quoted earlier, all patients appear to be on the right side of the supreme agent, G-D.

How did you draw the girl hitting the boy? Was the girl, who is the agent, to the left of the boy, the patient? And did the action take place from the left to the right?

In addition, if you are right-handed, when you drew that horizontal line with your right hand, did you also go from left to right?

Did you get the feeling after reading this that we are "all-right?"

Well, we are not. About ten percent of humans are left-handed. And no, it is not sinister to be left-handed. There may even be some advantages. First, if there were disadvantage to being left-handed, we might expect that over centuries, the incidence of left-handedness would change, but it appears it has not changed. Faurie and Ramond (2004) wanted to study the evolution of handedness. These investigators noted that during the upper Palaeolithic (ca. 35,000–10,000 BP), humans painted 'negative hands' by blowing pigments with a tube onto one hand applied on a stone wall while the tube was being held by the other hand. These paintings were found in caves in Western Europe. By examining the hand portrayed in these painting, the frequency of left versus right handers during this period could be assessed. For comparison, these investigators assessed the handedness of French university students by observing them perform the same task. These investigators found that there was no difference in the performance of this task, between these students and those people living in caves more than 10,000 year ago. Thus, it appears that left-handedness is neither evolving nor de-evolving.

Differences in brain organization should lead to differences in skills and behavior. Although studies have not revealed any significant difference between the intelligence of left- and right-handed people, there have been some reports about differences in creativity. One of the behaviors that has been and is still critical to humanity is creativity. In my book, *Creativity and the Brain*, I define creativity as the "ability to understand, develop and express new orderly relationships," or "being able to find and produce the thread that unites." Only about 10 percent of the population is left-handed; however, about 20 percent of Nobel Prize winners are left-handed. Although this would suggest that in general left-handers are more creative than right-handers, several Nobel Prizes are given out to people who performed work that was not necessarily creative, and I do not know how many left-handed Nobel Prize winners received their prize for their creativity.

G. Anthony Newland (1981) thought that since left-handed people are more challenged by their environment, which has been primarily organized for the right-handed people, they more often have to make special creative adaptations and this requirement may enhance their creativity. One of the first steps in creativity is what has been called divergent thinking, or more commonly called "thinking out of a box." One of the tests used to assess creative thinking is called the Torrance Tests of Creative Thinking. There are many forms of creativity including verbal and visuospatial. Newland used the Torrance Test of Visuospatial Creativity (figural test) to measure the creativity of 96 left-handed and 96 right-handed individuals. An analysis indicated that the left-handed participants demonstrated better divergent thinking than did the right-handers. Stanley Coren (1995) also found that left-handers are better at divergent thinking than are right-handers. The increased creativity found in left-handed people may be related to nurture (solving problems). In addition, even in most left-handers, it is their left hemisphere that mediates language and their right hemisphere that mediates visuospatial functions. Since left-handers use their left hand more than right-handers, their left hand, they be more likely to activate their right hemisphere. In addition, there may also be differences in brain development between left- and right-handers that could also account for this difference. Divergent thinking is primarily a function of the right hemisphere and there have been several functional imaging studies that appear to indicate that the frontal lobes are critical in this function.

Most of Albert Einstein's great creativity was in the visuospatial domain. Einstein wanted to be cremated but realized that scientists may want to see and examine his brain, so he gave permission to have his brain removed. Unfortunately, the pathologist who removed his brain cut it into more than 200 little squares and sent these pieces to people all over the world. Fortunately, he did take some pictures before he sliced Einstein's brain. In these photographs, it does appear that Einstein had large frontal lobes and his right frontal lobe does appear to be large. Some have speculated that Einstein was left-handed; however, there is little or no evidence that he was left-handed. Although Einstein wrote with his right hand, many left-handed people were taught to write with their right hand, but there are many other sources that claim he was right-handed. However, some of the greatest artists were left-handed, such as Leonardo da Vinci, Michelangelo, and Rubens. However, I could find no articles that compared the difference in the size of different portions of the frontal lobes in left- versus right-handers, as it pertains to creativity.

In addition to divergent thinking, convergent thinking is a critical element for creativity including the production of creative works. Coren (1995) found that right-handed participants appear to perform convergent thinking better than left-handed participants.

There are many sports where there is a higher percent of left-handers than there are in the general populations. There are many reasons for this increase. For example, since left-handedness is much less frequent than right-handedness, when a right-hander competes against a left-hander, the left-hander has more experience competing against right-handers than vice versa. In addition, almost all sports require the use of two hands, and in general, left-handers tend to be more ambidextrous than right-handers

Even in politics, of the last fifteen presidents seven have been left-handed (~47%), and none of them were sinister. Thus, being a left-hander is ALL-RIGHT.

2

UP

Introduction

In the first section, there was a discussion of the possible reasons why in the Bible and in our culture the right hand may be considered superior to the left. Also discussed was why it may be better to be on a person's right than on their left side. In the second section, the possible brain mechanisms for our right spatial bias are discussed. In the Bible and in our culture, there is another strong spatial bias, and that is upward. For example, heaven is up, hell is down. Elation is having high spirits-euphoria, being up-lifted and elevated. In contrast, depression is having low spirits, crestfallen, downcast, downhearted, and low-spirited. Like right-handedness and rightward spatial bias, the Bible has many statements about up and down. .

Psalm 107:26
They **went down to the depths**; Their soul melted away in their misery.

Isaiah 24:18
Then it will be that he who flees the report of disaster **will fall into the pit.**

Proverbs 15:24
The path of life leads **upward** for the wise… That he may keep away from Sheol **below.**

Proverbs 25:7
For it is better that it be said to you, "**Come up here**," Than for you to be **placed lower** in the presence of the prince, Whom your eyes have seen.

Luke 14:10
"But when you are invited, go and recline at the last place, so that when the one who has invited you comes, he may say to you, 'Friend, **move up higher'**; then you will have honor in the sight of all who are at the table with you.

DOI: 10.4324/9781003206682-3

Isaiah 60:1

"**Arise, shine**; for your light has come.

Ecclesiastes 3:21

Who knows that the breath of man **ascends** upward and the breath of the
beast descends downward to the earth?

Psalm 123:1

To You I lift up my eyes, O You who are enthroned in the heavens!

Isaiah 40:26

Lift up your eyes on high And see who has created these stars, The One who
leads forth their host by number, He calls them all by name; Because of the
greatness of His might and the strength of His power.

Daniel 4:34

"But at the end of that period, I, Nebuchadnezzar, raised my eyes toward
heaven and my reason returned to me, and I blessed the Most High and
praised and honored Him who lives forever.

John 11:41

So they removed the stone. Then Jesus raised His eyes, and said, "Father, I thank
You that You have heard Me.

There are many possible reasons why people consider that up is good and down
bad. Humans, animals, and even plants want and need light. Light, including sun-
light, most often comes from above. As children, we look up to our parents. When
we are sick, we are down in bed, when well, we are up. With death, many peoples'
body is put down into the ground, buried. But their souls go up to heaven.

Just as there are biological reasons for making right versus left decisions, perhaps
there are also biological reasons for down being negative and up being positive.
When people state they are "down," they are often expressing feelings of depression. The World Health Organization ranks major depressive disorder as one of
the major causes of prolonged disability. Although depression is a major cause of
disability and suffering, the pathophysiology of this disorder is still not fully understood. Depression is associated with signs and symptoms in many different domains,
including sleep, eating-appetite, energy, libido, as well as emotions and moods.

Many years ago, I was invited up to North Carolina to be a Visiting Professor
at the Department of Psychiatry at Duke University. They asked me to give a lecture about disorders of emotional communication. After giving this lecture, I had
lunch with several members of the Department of Psychiatry. During lunch, I was
asked the reasons why I had chosen to become a neurologist rather than a psychiatrist. I told them that my interest has always been in brain–behavior mechanisms
in both health and disease, but that I felt more comfortable with the means by
which neurologists reason about behavioral disorders than the means by which
psychiatrists perform their analyses. In addition, when I went to medical school, the
main therapy performed by psychiatrists was called non-directive psychotherapy.
I told them that I have no part of my brain that would allow me to be non-directive.

In addition, I am very impatient, and I would also be unable to sit eight or more hours a day listening to people complain.

One of the psychiatrists asked me to give an example of how neurologists and psychiatrists think differently about behavioral disorders. I ask them to name a psychiatric disease and this psychiatrist said "depression."

Clinicians have subtyped many different forms of depression and these different forms have some signs (observed behaviors) and symptoms (complaints) that vary. However, there are several critical features of almost all these forms of depression that are similar and these include a feeling of sadness, anhedonia (lack of pleasure), reduced energy with an increased fatigue, alterations in eating habits (most often a reduction of food intake), and a reduction in sexual activity. In addition, patients with depression often spend an increased amount of their time with internally generated thoughts rather than external interactions.

I mentioned to these psychiatrists that certainly depression can be brought on by external factors, but the factors that induce depression cannot account for most of the signs and symptoms of depression. I told them that I recalled reading that when Freud wrote about depression, he suggested that this mood disorder is often a response to a loss, such as the loss of a loved one or a failure to achieve a goal. Furthermore, he thought that a person's unconscious anger weakens that person's ego and this weakening results in self-hate that becomes manifest as depression. However, weakening of the ego cannot explain the brain mechanisms that account for the signs and symptoms of depression.

Then another psychiatrist asked me about the serotonin hypothesis. I mentioned that the serotonin hypothesis was a post hoc hypothesis and that post hoc hypotheses, unlike tested a priori hypotheses, are often incorrect explanations. In 1952 there were new medications being developed for the treatment of tuberculosis (TB). One of the medications they were trying to use to treat this disease is called iproniazid. This medication is a derivative of isoniazid, another medication that was being used to treat patients with TB. It was noted that during the attempted treatment of TB with iproniazid, several depressed patients taking this medication had an improvement in their mood. While isoniazid was, and is, one of the most effective medications for the treatment of TB, iproniazid was found not to be effective against TB but was found to be a strong antidepressant.

Another medication, called tranylcypromine, which was designed to be used as a nasal decongestant, was found to also be an antidepressant. Investigators also found that both these medications inhibited the enzyme monoamine oxidase (MAOI). This enzyme normally breaks down neurotransmitters such as norepinephrine and serotonin, and thereby increase the levels of these neurotransmitters in the brain. These MAOIs were the first class of antidepressants to be developed. Now they are not commonly used because they have dangerous interactions with certain foods and numerous other medications. On the basis of these observations, however, psychiatrists proposed that depression was caused by low levels of these neurotransmitters. I explained to the psychiatrists, with whom I was speaking, that although these transmitters might be low in people with depression and increasing the level of these neurotransmitters might help depression, this neurotransmitter hypothesis does not explain why the levels of serotonin and norepinephrine are low in people with depression and why low levels of these neurotransmitters would induce the signs and symptoms of depression.

Then another psychiatrist asked, "Well Ken, how would a neurologist explain depression?

I mentioned to them the means by which neurologists' reason was strongly influenced by the works of James Hughlings Jackson, a British neurologist who did his work in the late 19th and early 20th centuries. Hughlings Jackson was very influenced by Charles Darwin's book the *Origin of Species*, which was published in 1859. Hughlings Jackson posited that the human brain reflects the evolutionary history of animals. With evolution the brain developed a progressively greater ability to store a repertoire of knowledge and behaviors that enhance the animal's ability to successfully interact with its environment. Hughlings Jackson, however, also noted that in order to perform these more complex interactions with the environment, the more evolutionarily primitive portions of the brain that are more likely to program more stereotypic behaviors must be inhibited. According to Hughlings Jackson, with injury to the cerebral cortex, which is the phylogenetically most advanced portions of the human brain, there is not only a loss of higher forms of knowledge and behaviors but also a release of more phylogenetically primitive behaviors.

For example, when I tell a healthy person to keep their eyes open and I repeatedly tap their forehead with my index finger, they will blink once or twice. This blinking of the eyelid is a protective reflex. However, if I keep tapping, normal people will stop blinking. The frontal lobes are important in inhibiting meaningless actions. If a patient has frontal lobe injury-dysfunction when I continue tapping, they will continue blinking because they no longer can inhibit this primitive protective reflex.

I suggested to these psychiatrists that since depression normally comes on when there is a loss of a family member, a loss of health, or a failure to succeed at an endeavor, it is possible that depression is a phylogenically more primitive behavioral state whose role is to help preserve resources during times when well-being or even their life might be in jeopardy, not from an attack, but from deprivation.

Hibernation

When I was in grammar school, like many other children, I learned that when winter came, animals, such as bears, who do not migrate to warmer climates, go to sleep in a cave and wake up when spring comes. We were told that this state is called hibernation. I subsequently learned that during hibernation many animals, such as bears, might not sleep all the time but are very inactive and have a reduction of their metabolic activities. Thus, some call this state "torpor." When these animals are in this state of torpor they do not explore, do not play, and do not engage in sexual activities. During winter, little or no food is available to these animals and even with a reduction of their activity and a lower metabolic rate, these animals still lose a tremendous amount of weight. They lose all this weight because even though they have less need for nutrients that supply energy, they have no caloric intake and their bodies still require energy. If they were not in a state of torpor-hibernation, they would have insufficient energy stores to survive.

When humans learn they are seriously ill, lose a family member, or are a failure and unsuccessful, their brains might shift them into a survival mode and this survival mode might be similar to the state of torpor that bears use to survive during the winter. Just like bears, humans who suffer a loss, ill health, or failure will curtail their exploratory activities, retreat to an environment that requires a minimum of external (allocentric) attention and interactions with environmental stimuli, have difficulty finding activities that they enjoy, decrease their sexual activities, and alter their sleeping as well as eating habits. This state is called "depression."

With hibernation in bears, and with melancholic major depression in humans, there are similar changes in the body such as a loss of weight, an increased concentration of serum cortisol, a decrease in certain neurotransmitter levels, and changes in cyclic-adenosine monophosphate-binding activity.

Although following a loss or a failure a temporary state of depression is normal, many individuals enter this state even when there is no loss, when the loss is trivial or imagined or after normally entering this state, many people have an inability to exit this state this state of depression.

The reason why some people suffer with depressive disorders and others do not is not entirely known. Some psychological theories include 'learned helplessness,' or a person's belief that they cannot control the outcomes of important events. However, the cause of depression might be, in part, be genetic. For example, concordance studies of identical twins versus siblings have revealed that if one twin has depression, the other twin will be more than three times more likely to have depression than a sibling who is not an identical twin. These observations suggest that depression, at least in part, has a biological cause. That depressive disorders might be in part biological does not mean, as mentioned earlier, that environmental factors do play an important role in depression.

Neurotransmitters

The brain networks that induce these alterations of behavior are not entirely known. One of the means by which we can begin to understand the pathophysiology of this neuropsychiatric disorder is to study patients who manifest this depressive behavior as part of a neurological disease. Depression can be seen in several neurological diseases, including a hemispheric stroke that damages the frontal lobe, as well as degenerative diseases such as Parkinson's disease. When people get depressed, they are given medication that increases a brain neurotransmitter called serotonin. The reason increasing the brain's serotonin help depression is still not fully known. However, patients with Parkinson's disease have a loss of the cells in a part of their brain stem, called the raphe nucleus, and it is this nucleus that provides the brain with serotonin. Patients with Parkinson's disease have loss of neurons in another brain stem nucleus, called the locus coeruleus. This nucleus provides the brain with norepinephrine and the substantia nigra that supplies the brain with dopamine.

One of the first medication to treat people with psychosis was reserpine. Although now there have been some debates about this, reserpine, which blocks these neurotransmitters, frequently appeared to cause depression. Therefore, it was thought that there is a relationship between depression and a reduction of these neurotransmitters, especially serotonin and norepinephrine. When medications that increased the brain serotonin, such as citalopram (Celexa), escitalopram (Lexapro), fluoxetine (Prozac), paroxetine (Paxil), and sertraline (Zoloft) were developed, they were very successful in treating people with depression. In addition, other medications for depression, such as desvenlafaxine (Pristiq), duloxetine (Cymbalta), and venlafaxine (Effexor) increase both serotonin and norepinephrine levels in the brain and have also been successful in treating many people with depression. Although these observations support the neurotransmitter postulate of depression, this postulate, however, does not explain the behavioral manifestations of depression.

Studies of animals have demonstrated that during the state of torpor-hibernation the majority of the brain is hypoactive. After visual, auditory, and tactile stimuli enter the brain, before reaching the cortex, they go through a relay station deep in the brain and these incoming sensory neurons connect with the neurons that go to the cerebral cortex. However, there are also inhibitory neurons that meet with these sensory neurons and when these inhibitory neurons are active, they prevent these sensory neurons from sending sensory information to the primary sensory cortex. Thus, the activity of these inhibitory neurons can put the cerebral cortex in a dark cave.

Default Network

One of the new techniques that have allowed neuroscientists and clinicians to make advances in understanding brain functions in health and brain dysfunction during a disease is functional imaging. When a certain part of the brain is performing an activity, the neurons in this part of the brain become very active and this increase in activity requires a greater requirement for energy. The fuel for brain energy is glucose and oxygen. These fuels are brought to the active neurons in the brain by the blood. Therefore, when a part of the brain increases it activity, it usually requires more blood and functional imaging measures the changes of blood flow. Earlier, the means of measuring blood flow was by injecting a radioactive material into the brain and then measuring the radioactivity in different portions of the brain. Positron emission tomography, or PET, is one example of this technique. More recently, clinicians and investigators have been using functional magnetic resonance imaging (fMRI). The blood carrying oxygen has different magnetic properties than the blood leaving an active area where the oxygen had been used, and the fMRI can now detect this change. Prior to functional imaging, and structural brain imaging such as CT or MRI, the methods used to determine the specific functions of the brain were to examine patients who had brain damage from some disease, such as stroke, and after the patient died, to perform a post mortem examination of their brain and see what was damaged. One of the earliest examples of this was Paul Broca, who reported his patient who could only say the word, "tan," but who could comprehend other peoples' speech. When this patient died Broca found that his left lower frontal lobe was injured. With structural imaging such as MRI or CT, we are now able to learn what area of the brain is damaged, even in patients who are still alive.

Investigators who were performing functional imaging of healthy participants, to learn the parts of the brain that activate when participants perform some form of perceptual, cognitive, or motor task, often had to use a control condition. In this control condition, the subjects were blindfolded and wore earplugs. In these conditions, the participants were not externally stimulated nor were they asked to perform any task. However, while remaining in the waking state, these participants were able to think, recall, and plan. In some manner, this functional imaging procedure is like being in a cave. During this experimental condition, when brain activities are of a self-referential nature, investigators found that across subjects the same brain areas showed activation. Investigators using this technique called this self-activated network the default network (Buckner et al., 2007; Raichle et al., 2001). This default network includes the ventromedial prefrontal cortex, the anterior cingulate gyrus, the lateral parietal cortex, as well as portions of the limbic system including the hippocampus and the amygdala (Figures 2.1 and 2.2).

When investigators request that their healthy control participants lie down in a scanner, and prevent these subjects from receiving any type of sensory stimuli as well as having them avoid moving, they are, perhaps, asking these participants, at least in part, to replicate a state of torpor. Functional imaging studies of patients with depression have also revealed that this default network is very active.

There are many means by which depression can be treated including medicines such as serotonin agonists (selective serotonin reuptake inhibitors), serotonin and norepinephrine agonists (serotonin and norepinephrine uptake inhibitors), tricyclic antidepressants, psychotherapy, electric convulsive therapy (ECT), magnetic stimulation of the brain, and vagus nerve stimulation. When peoples' depression is successfully treated and they undergo functional imaging, the function of this default network returns to normal (Sheline et al., 2009).

Studies of patients with focal hemispheric injuries, such as stroke, using functional imaging have suggested that different emotions appear to be mediated by different parts of the brain. As mentioned earlier, one of the first reports that suggested that different emotions may in part be mediated by different parts of the brain was written by Babinski (1914). He noted that individuals with a right-hemispheric lesion often appear indifferent or even inappropriately euphoric. Subsequently, Hecaen, Ajuriagurra, and de Massonet (1951) and Denny-Brown et al. (1952) also reported that patients with a right hemisphere stroke were often

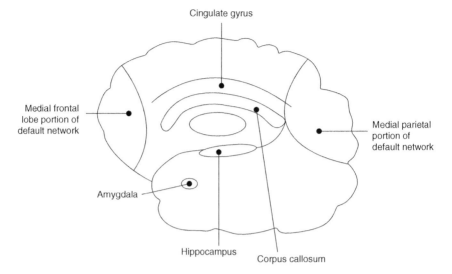

FIGURE 2.1 A Medial Portions of the Default Network

When investigators at Washington University were studying functional imaging (positron emission tomography) and wanted to learn those areas of the brain that increased their activity when performing certain activities, they needed to compare what happens during this activity compared to a resting state. They, therefore, imaged healthy participants while they were blindfolded, not hearing speech or music, and not working on any problems. They noted that the parts of the brain that were more toward the middle appear to be activated, such as the posterior cingulate cortex, the precuneus, the medial prefrontal cortex, and the parietal lobes. During this time, these participants were thinking about personal information, autobiographical memories, future plans, and goals.

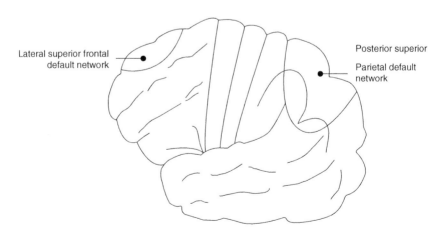

FIGURE 2.2 The Lateral Portions of the Default Network

inappropriately indifferent. Gainotti (1972) studied a large group of patients with lateralized brain damage and reported that those patients with right hemisphere lesions often appeared to be indifferent about their disability.

These reports suggest that when the left hemisphere is injured, the right hemisphere is disinhibited and mediates the negative emotions of anxiety and sadness. In contrast, when the right hemisphere is injured, it releases the left hemisphere that mediates positive emotions. However, many patients with right hemisphere disease, such as stroke, exhibit unawareness of the left side of their body and thus they are often not aware that they have weakness and had a stroke. This disorder is called anosognosia (a = without, noso = disease, gnosia = knowledge). Some neurologists thought that it is anosognosia that may be responsible for this right–left hemispheric difference in emotional response.

Patients with uncontrollable seizures can sometimes be helped by removal of the part of the brain where these seizures start. However, before operating on the brain and removing a portion of the brain, it is important to know the functions of each hemisphere. One of the means by which the physician learns about laterality of a hemisphere's functions in these patients is by putting each hemisphere asleep by injecting a barbiturate into the carotid artery on one side. Each carotid artery supplies blood to almost the entire hemisphere. After these patients recover from this hemispheric anesthesia, physicians inject a barbiturate into the carotid artery on the opposite side and inactivate the other hemisphere (the Wada test).

As mentioned earlier, Terzian (1964) as well as Rossi and Rosadini (1967) studied the emotional reactions of patients undergoing Wada testing. They observed that with right carotid injections of a barbiturate, which anesthetizes the right hemisphere, patients often experienced and exhibited what appeared to be emotional euphoria.

Another experiment...before you read the next paragraph. If you have a piece of large blank white paper (e.g., eight and one half by eleven inches), put the paper on the table such that its horizontal, with the eleven-inch side parallel to your body. Now draw a straight line, that is about 9 inches long, in the center of the paper, so that this line is about one inch from each end of the paper. Then make a mark at the center on this line. After you do this, bend the two ends of the paper so that beginning of the line and the end of the line meet on this folded paper. The fold crease should be at the center of the line. Now, look to see if the mark you made was at the center of the line or deviated to one or the other side.

The right hemisphere of the human brain primarily attends to left side of body-centered hemispace and the left hemisphere primarily attends to the right side of space. When healthy adults are presented with a long horizontal line (e.g., nine inches) and are asked to mark the middle of the line, they often tend to deviate their attempted bisections to the left of the center, a phenomenon known as pseudoneglect (e.g., Bowers & Heilman, 1980; McCourt & Jewell, 1999). Subsequent research has suggested that this left-sided deviation is related to right-hemispheric dominance in the allocation of spatial attention.

You are probably tired of reading about these experiments, but here is another line bisection test. Please get a clean sheet of paper and draw the line, as you had for the experiment you just did. But this time, before you attempt to bisect this line, place it vertically, so the bottom of the line is toward the floor and the top toward the ceiling. Please keep the middle of this sheet of paper about eye level. Now again attempt to make a mark in the center of this line (bisect the line). After you attempt to bisect this vertical line, please fold it as you did before (both ends of the line meeting) and see if your mark deviated upward or downward.

Healthy individuals often also display a vertical attentional bias. When attempting to bisect vertically oriented lines, they often deviate upward (Jeerakathil & Kirk, 1994). It is possible that this upward bias may also be related to hemispheric asymmetries. When performing the line bisection task, individuals need to see the entire line, thus they need to initially engage global attention. Studies have revealed that the right hemisphere appears to be dominant in mediating global attention (Fink et al., 1996). In addition, other studies have revealed that the right hemisphere, when compared to the left, appears to have an upward attentional bias (Mańkowska et al., 2018; Suavansri et al., 2012). Thus, the right hemisphere's dominance in the mediation of global spatial attention, as well as the right hemisphere's bias toward allocating attention leftward, would explain both horizontal and vertical pseudoneglect.

Several functional imaging studies performed on patients with depression suggested the left hemisphere appears to be hypoactive (Bench et al., 1992; Phelps et al., 1984; Bruder et al., 2017). Since there is a relative increase in the activation of the right compared to their left, hemisphere that is associated with a depressed mood, people with depression may have an increase in their leftward and upward attentional bias. However, studies of individuals with depression performing the horizontal line bisection test did not reveal an increase in their leftward deviation (Cavézian et al., 2007; Ramos-Brieva et al., 1984). In addition, if, with depression, there was an increase of the upward attentional bias, why would all the metaphors about depression be downward?

There is, however, another possibility, based on the organization of the brain, that may help explain why when we are sad or depressed we feel down. Information from the retina, in the back of the eye, goes to the back of the brain, the occipital cortex. This area is called the primary visual cortex. When light falls on a different part of the retina, specific neurons in the primary visual cortex become active and this allows this primary cortex to develop the configuration of what is being seen. Subsequently, these patterns of neuronal activity are further processed by visual association areas. This visual processing appears to be performed primarily by two networks (Figure 2.3). One of these networks is in the lower (ventral) part of occipital lobe and also partly in the lower part of the posterior temporal lobe. This is called the ventral network. The other network is higher up in the brain (dorsal) and includes the dorsal part of the occipital lobe and the posterior part of the parietal lobe, the dorsal network. Blood to the ventral portions of temporal and occipital lobes is supplied by the posterior cerebral arteries and blood to the parietal lobes

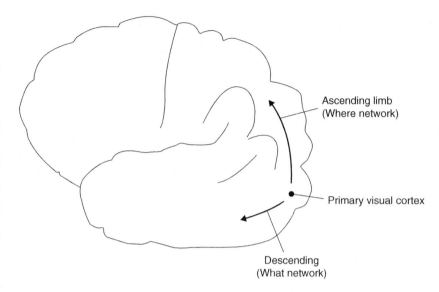

Ascending limb
(Where network)

Primary visual cortex

Descending
(What network)

FIGURE 2.3 Visual Association Cortex

After the visual information comes to the primary visual cortex in the occipital lobe, these stimuli are then processed by two different networks. One is toward the bottom of the brain (ventral) and is important for the recognition of objects. This has been called the "what" stream. The second network is higher up and is important in determining the location of objects, and therefore, has been called the "where" stream.

is supplied by branches of the middle cerebral artery. Most often when patients get a stroke, it is in one artery, and thus, patients with strokes may injure just their dorsal occipital and parietal lobes or the ventral portions of their temporal and occipital lobes.

In 1890, Lissauer reported that individuals who had injured their ventral visual network (Figure 2.3) could still see objects and could also locate these objects in space. However, these patients could not visually recognize the objects they were viewing, but if they felt the object, they could then recognize the object. Sigmund Freud called this disorder visual agnosia (a = without, gnosia = knowledge).

In contrast, Balint (1909) reported that individuals who had injured their dorsal (upper) visual system (including the parietal lobes) could visually recognize objects (unlike the individuals with ventral injury with visual agnosia), but they had trouble spatially locating the object in relation to their body. Many decades later, doing research with monkeys, Ungerleider and Mishkin (1982) also found that the monkeys with a ventral occipital-temporal lesion had trouble visually recognizing objects and those with dorsal parietal-occipital lesion had trouble locating objects. These results were similar to those reported by Lissauer (1890) and Balint (1909). Ungerleider and Mishkin (1982) called the ventral system, which is important in visually recognizing objects, the "what" system, and the dorsal system, which is important in determining the location of objects, the "where" system.

There appears to be a second difference between these dorsal and ventral visual processing networks that involve the spatial allocation of attention. Patients with right parietal lesions often show the signs and symptoms of a neurological disorder called unilateral spatial neglect (see Heilman et al., 2012 for a review). These patients appear to be unaware of stimuli that are present on the left side of their body. When presented with a horizontal line and asked to place a mark in the center of the line (bisect the line), they misplace the mark to the right, because they are relatively unaware of the extent of the left side of the line. If they are given a sheet of paper with lines randomly distributed over this paper and asked to cross out all the lines, patients with neglect will often fail to cancel the lines on the left side of the paper. When performing the line bisection test or the cancellation test, if the paper is moved to the right side of the body, patients perform better, and if moved to the left, they deviate even more to the right. Therefore, damage to this more dorsal visual network appears to cause spatial inattention-unawareness neglect that is body-centered (egocentric).

Chatterjee (1994) proposed that an object in the environment may be represented in the brain by its location in relation to the viewer (viewer centered or egocentric) or it may be represented by its own intrinsic spatial properties. He wanted to learn if patients with left-sided spatial neglect fail to be aware of (attend to) stimuli on their left side (viewer centered) or if they fail to attend to the left side of objects independent of their location in respect to the viewer's head and body. Four of his patients demonstrated viewer-centered (egocentric) neglect and three demonstrated object-centered (allocentric) neglect. Chatterjee's report revealed that viewer-centered and object-centered reference frames are functionally dissociable.

Medina et al. (2009) presented a battery of tests to 171 participants to learn the localization of lesions that induced body-centered (egocentric) versus object-centered neglect. These patients were given tests designed to disambiguate between body-centered (egocentric neglect) and object-centered (allocentric neglect). For example, they presented a cancellation test with a sheet of paper (Figure 2.4). On this paper were 10 complete circles, 10 circles with gaps on the left, and 10 circles with gaps on the right (Figure 2.4). All these circles were randomly distributed on this paper. Participants were instructed to cross out the circles with the gaps. This test was administered at midline of the patient's body. Patients with body-centered (egocentric) neglect (inattention) would fail to cancel circles with openings on one side of their body (Figure 2.5). Those with allocentric neglect would fail to cancel those circles with opening on one side, independent of their location in respect to their head and body (Figure 2.6). They found that those patients with injury to portions of the dorsal stream of visual processing, including the right inferior parietal lobe, revealed egocentric neglect (inattention). In contrast, patients with allocentric neglect had injury of the ventral stream, including the posterior inferior temporal gyrus. These results suggest that portions of the dorsal stream of visual processing, including the right inferior parietal lobe, are involved in allocating spatial attention in body-centered (egocentric) coordinates. In contrast, portions of

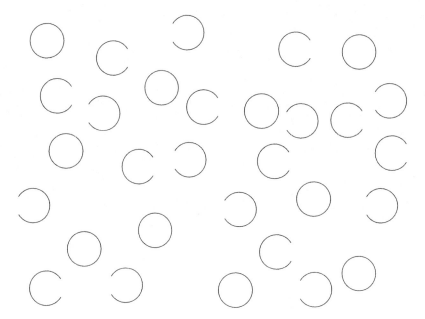

FIGURE 2.4 Cancellation Test

In this test, a paper is placed on the table directly in front of the seated patient. On this paper, there are 30 circles, with 10 being full circles, 10 having openings (a gap) on the left side, and 10 with a gap on the right side.

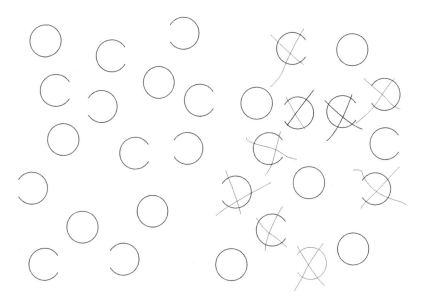

FIGURE 2.5 The Egocentric Neglect The performance of a patient with body centered (egocentric) neglect from a right hemisphere parietal stroke.

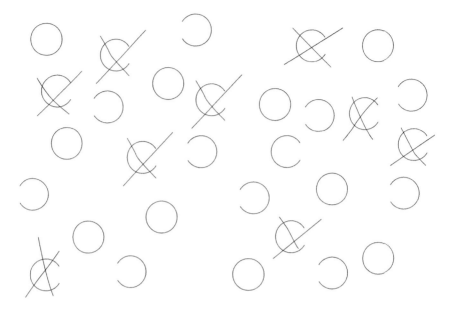

FIGURE 2.6 Allocentric Neglect

The performance of a patient with object centered (allocentric) neglect from a right temporal lobe stroke.

the ventral stream (including the posterior inferior temporal gyrus) are involved in allocating object-centered (allocentric) attention.

In addition to the ventral–dorsal visual network dichotomies for "what versus where," and the ventral–dorsal dichotomy of "object-centered (allocentric) versus body-centered (egocentric) inattention (neglect)," there is a third important ventral-dorsal dichotomy. There have been reports of patients who had strokes to the ventral temporal-occipital cortex, usually caused by thrombosis of the posterior cerebral artery, that produces neglect of upper space, and patients who had a stroke in their middle cerebral artery distribution that injured their parietal lobe and dorsal occipital cortex had neglect of lower space (Ergun-Marterer et al., 2001; Pitzalis et al., 1997; Rapcsak et al., 1988; Shelton et al., 1990). These studies suggest that the ventral visual network allocates vertical attention upward, and the dorsal visual network allocates vertical attention downward.

Different forms of visual cognitive activities may be able to asymmetrically engage-activate these two vertical attentional networks. To test the hypothesis that activation of the ventral visual stream will induce an upward attentional bias, Claunch et al (2012) had healthy, right-handed individuals perform vertical line bisections. Patients who have had a thrombosis of the posterior cerebral artery often have damage to the lower (ventral) part of the occipital lobe, as well as the ventral temporal lobe, on one side of the brain. This damaged part of the brain is called the "What" area. If it is the right posterior cerebral artery that is clotted and

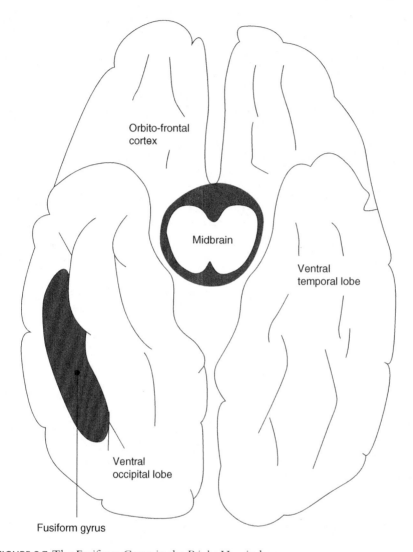

Orbito-frontal
cortex

Midbrain

Ventral
temporal lobe

Ventral
occipital lobe

Fusiform gyrus

FIGURE 2.7 The Fusiform Gyrus in the Right Hemisphere

The fusiform gyrus is on the bottom of the temporal lobe. Injury to this fusiform
gyrus is associated with a loss of facial recognition, known as prosopagnosia.

the right ventral temporal and occipital areas are damaged, people often lose their
ability to know "What" or whose face they are viewing. Since face recognition is
performed by the ventral visual network, primarily the fusiform gyrus, which is
located on the bottom of the temporal lobe (Figure 2.7), when performing these
line bisections, pictures of famous faces were presented either above or below these
vertical lines. The participants who performed these vertical line bisections were
asked to recognize and remember the face they viewed while they performed the
line bisections. In control trials, there were no faces. An analysis of these healthy

participants' performance revealed an upward bias in all of the conditions. This upward bias, however, was significantly greater during the face recognition and face recall conditions than in the control condition. Because face recognition is mediated by the fusiform gyrus in the right inferior temporal and occipital lobes (Figure 2.7), this increase in upward bias was attributed to an increase in activation of the ventral attentional network (Claunch et al., 2012).

Certain emotions may be able to asymmetrically activate-engage the ventral-object-centered (allocentric) visual network and other emotions may asymmetrically activate the dorsal-egocentric visual network. For example, emotions such as surprise and joy/happiness may induce an attentional state where a person's attention is directed outward, so they can attend to specific items in the environment (allocentric attention) (Hillis et al., 2005). When attending to specific items in the environment, the ventral-allocentric system should be more activated than the dorsal-egocentric system. However, when a person experiences emotions and moods such as sadness and depression, their attention is often directed inward (egocentric attention) with greater activation of the default network allowing them to listen to their own speech, to view self-generated images, and to retrieve memories. In addition, studies have revealed that depression can be associated with a failure to normally down-regulate activity in the default network (Sheline et al., 2009). These findings provide us with sufficient information to propose a brain network that may be important in the mediation of the signs and symptoms of depression. With depression, the dorsal-egocentric system would be more activated than the ventral-allocentric system and activation of this dorsal network would induce a propensity to allocate attention downward.

Drago, Heilman, and Foster (2010) asked 20 healthy individuals to mark a large sheet of paper, in any place of their choosing, after they retrieved seven types of emotional memories. The authors found that the memories of different emotional experiences were associated with different spatial placements of these marks. With positive emotional memories, the participants placed their marks higher than they placed their marks with negative emotional memories.

The results of the study by Drago et al. suggest that people who frequently experience sad emotions or depression are more likely to allocate their attention downward. In contrast, those individuals who more frequently experience joy and happy emotions may be more likely to allocate their attention upward. Until recently, the relationships between the spatial allocation of vertical attention mediated by the ventral visual network and the dorsal visual network—and emotional processing—have been comparatively unexplored. We (Aleksandra Mańkowska, Michał Harciarek, & Kenneth M. Heilman, 2020) tested the hypothesis that mood disposition, as measured by the number of depressive symptoms experienced by an individual, would affect the allocation of vertical attention. We used the Hospital Anxiety and Depression Scale to evaluate depressive symptoms in 48 right-handed men and women. To be included, the individuals had to be right-handed; with normal, or corrected-to-normal, vision, hearing, and normal performance on the Mini-Mental State Examination (Folstein et al., 1975).

Individuals were excluded if they had any serious chronic medical, neurological, or psychiatric disorders, as well as current alcohol or drug abuse, or were currently taking psychoactive medication.

In this study, the participants were asked to mark the center of (bisect) 24 vertical lines that were 24 centimeters long. These lines were located centrally on sheets of paper. The sheets of paper were presented consecutively in the vertical (coronal) plane such that the center of the line was at eye level and within an arm's reach. During this task, the participants were not given any feedback.

We found that overall, these participants deviated their bisections of vertical lines upward; however, the number of depressive symptoms experienced by an individual significantly correlated to the magnitude of the vertical bias, such that the higher the score on the depression scale, the lower the bisection. These results do therefore support the hypothesis that the propensity to experience depressive moods may be associated with a relative lowering of the vertical attentional bias.

In patients with depression, there is elevated connectivity in the default network (Kaiser et al., 2015) as well as reduced connectivity within frontoparietal control systems involved external attention. This change in the balance between these two networks may account for the depressive biases toward internal thoughts at the cost of engaging with the external world. Studies of depressed individuals have also revealed that with rumination (repetitive self-generated thoughts—a form of egocentric attention), there is an increased activity within the default mode network (Burkhouse et al., 2017; van Wingen et al., 2014), which includes the parietal lobes.

Since the parietal lobes spatially allocate attention downward, and with depression, there may be an increase in parietal lobe activation, this parietal lobe activation may be inducing a relative downward alteration in the allocation of vertical attention. However, this study did not measure ruminative thinking directly and further studies are needed to investigate this hypothesis. Future research should also evaluate individuals with mood disorders such as clinical depression, as these disorders may reveal a stronger vertical attentional bias than individuals with out depressive symptoms.

Whereas the entire reason why, in many languages, emotions and moods associated with happiness or sadness are verbally expressed by using vertical spatial metaphors is not known, the possibility that we explored is that with moods and emotional experiences, such as depression and sadness, there is an alteration of the vertical allocation of attention.

Finally, it might also be worthwhile to study whether alterations in an individual's propensity to allocate attention upward and allocentrically might improve their depressed mood.

3

APPROACH–STAY–LEAVE

Introduction

Just as the Bible mentions rightward and upward, there are also many portions of the Bible that mention going forward. The following are some examples:

Isaiah 43:18
Remember ye not the former things, neither consider the things of old.

Psalms 32:8
I will instruct thee and teach thee in the way which thou shalt go: I will guide thee with mine eye.

Exodus 14:15–16
And the LORD said unto Moses, Wherefore criest thou unto me? speak unto the children of Israel, that they go forward:

Isaiah 43:18–19
Remember ye not the former things, neither consider the things of old.

Corinthians 5:17
Therefore if any man [be] in Christ, [he is] a new creature: old things are passed away; behold, all things are become new.

Deuteronomy 1:6
The LORD our God spoke unto us in Horeb, saying, Ye have dwelt long enough in this mount:

John 5:8
Jesus saith unto him, Rise, take up thy bed, and walk.

Proverbs 4:25
Let thine eyes look right on, and let thine eyelids look straight before thee.

DOI: 10.4324/9781003206682-4

In general, there are four major conditions that motivate actions. The first is biological, people need food and water. They need to stay warm, but not too hot; they need to avoid stimuli that cause pain and injury. The second major motivation for actions is that people go forward and perform activities because they are rewarded and will remain as well as continue these activities if they continue to be rewarded. They may leave when they are no longer being rewarded. Third, most animals, especially humans, learn that they must go forward and perform activities (anticipation) that will increase the probability that in the future they, their families, their friends, and their colleagues will survive, be rewarded, and have positive emotional experiences. The fourth is emotions, which are strongly related to anticipatory behaviors. Emotions, such as joy and even anger, motivate us to move forward, while fear, sadness, and disgust motivate us to move backward-away. In the following sections, we will discuss what happens in the brain that entices us to go forward or come back, stay, or leave, based on reward, anticipation, and emotions.

Reward

As mentioned, one of the major symptoms of depression is anhedonia, a lack of joy, happiness, pleasure, or reward. In the 1930s, B.F. Skinner, a famous behavioral psychologist, developed an experimental cage or box where he trained animals such as rats. This "Skinner Box" had the ability to train the animal to behave in a certain manner with stimuli. The animal could be trained to press a lever when a light came on. If the light came on and the animal pressed the lever, the animal would receive a food reward. However, if no light came on and the animal pressed the lever, there would be no reward. Behavioral psychologists also used this experimental design to study humans. They learned that if a behavior was rewarded, the animal or human would continue to perform this behavior. In contrast, if a behavior was not rewarded, the human or animal would rapidly learn to stop performing that behavior. When the light came on and the participant pressed the lever, but this behavior was only randomly rewarded, then animals and people would continue to perform this activity and when the rewards stopped, they would take longer to learn that this activity was useless and to stop this activity.

Olds and Milner (1954) wanted to learn what parts of the brain mediate the rewarding effects that drive animals and people to continue rewarded behavior. They inserted electrodes into a variety of regions of the rat brain and then placed these rodents in a Skinner Box. When these animals pushed a lever in the Skinner Box, an electrical charge would be delivered to the portion of the animal's brain where these electrodes were placed and this electrical charge would active the adjacent portions of the brain. When performing these experiments, Olds and Milner noted that when the animal pressed a lever that stimulated the region of the brain near the septal nuclei, something very unusual happened. The animals who were getting this brain stimulation with lever pressing did not get any form of an external reward, like food or water. Although they did not get food or something to drink, they continued to press this lever. Their desire to press the lever and have an electrical current sent to this region of the brain was so strong that even when they were hungry and thirsty and food and water was available, they chose to press this lever rather than eat the food or drink the water.

About the same time as Olds and Milner performed their studies on rats, Robert Heath, a neurologist at Tulane University in New Orleans, was putting similar electrodes in the brain of humans and was targeting the same area, the region of the septal nucleus. According to *The 3-Pound Universe*, by Judith Hooper and Dick Teres, Robert Heath stated, "By implanting electrodes… we were able to localize the brain's pleasure … systems. We'd interview a patient about pleasant subjects and see the pleasure system firing… The pleasure system includes the septal area."

Robert Heath placed electrodes in patients who had a variety of psychiatric diseases. He noted that some of these patients appeared to be miserable; however, with stimulation they seemed to be happy and would smile. Dr. Heath asked one woman who was receiving this treatment why she was smiling. She answered, "I don't know … Are you doing something to me? [Giggles.] I don't usually sit around and laugh at nothing. I must be laughing at something." "What in the hell are you doing?" she asked. "You must be hitting some goody place." According to Heath the "goody place" is the septal pleasure center.

Scientists now know that the region of the brain where Olds and Milner placed these electrodes probably activated a cluster of neurons, which are very close to the septal region. The critical groups of neurons in this network are called the nucleus accumbens and the ventral striatum. More recently, at our University of Florida Health Center, Michael Okun et al. (2004) inserted electrodes in the region of the nucleus accumbens of a patient with obsessive-compulsive disorder. During stimulation, the patient consistently developed a smile and also became euphoric.

The reason why activation of this nucleus accumbens is pleasant and rewarding is not entirely known. The nucleus accumbens, however, is part of an anatomically distributed circuit known as the ventral striatum (Ikemoto & Panksepp, 1999) (Figure 3.1). It receives inputs from three major areas of the brain: (1) prefrontal lobes, including the ventromedial area that when stimulated has been reported to help relieve depression; (2) olfactory tubercle, which receives information from the olfactory neurons that detect smells, such as food, and might be important in sexual attraction via pheromones; and (3) the mesolimbic dopamine system. The neurons of this system have their cell bodies in a part of the midbrain called the mesencephalon. These cells are found in a middle part of the midbrain called the ventral tegmental area. These neurons that go from the midbrain to the nucleus accumbens give off the neurotransmitter dopamine. It is the excretion of this neurotransmitter that activates the nucleus accumbens and provides the experience of reward.

The nucleus accumbens sends neurons to other nuclei called the ventral pallidum and from there to a portion of the thalamus called the dorsomedial nucleus, and this thalamic nucleus is strongly connected to the frontal lobes.

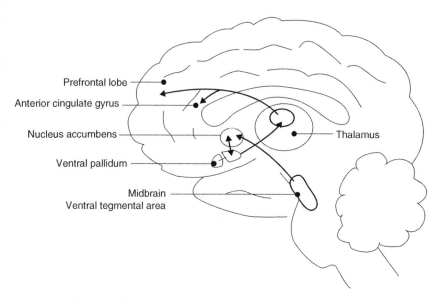

FIGURE 3.1 The Reward Network

The nucleus accumbens lies deep under the frontal lobes called the basal forebrain. It receives dopaminergic inputs from the ventral tegmental area that is located in the midbrain. The connection between the ventral tegmental area and the nucleus accumbens is called mesolimbic pathway. These dopaminergic neurons excite neurons within the nucleus accumbens.

The output neurons from the nucleus accumbens go to the basal ganglia (the ventral portion of the globus pallidus), also known as the ventral striatum or ventral pallidum. This basal ganglia projects to the medial dorsal nucleus of the dorsal thalamus, which in turn projects to the prefrontal cortex and the anterior portion of the cingulate gyrus.

It is not known how the nucleus accumbens mediates reward. However, the frontal lobes are responsible for determining long-term goals and for activating the motor system in pursuit of these goals. This frontal–nucleus accumbens–ventral pallidum–dorsomedial thalamus–frontal loop might act as a feedback loop such that when a goal is accomplished this loop provides positive feedback to the frontal lobe executive system, "goal accomplished."

Using fMRI to examine regional hemodynamic responses, it was found that people with depression had attenuated responses in the ventral striatum during reward-processing tasks. Dunn et al. (2002) reported that there was a correlation between a psychomotor retardation with anhedonia and lower metabolism in the ventral striatum. Furthermore, Epstein et al. (2006) found that when compared to normal people, patients with depression demonstrate less ventral striatal activation to positive stimuli and that this decrease of activation correlates with a decrease of interest and pleasure from performing activities.

Anticipatory Activities

Although we often perform behaviors that lead to an immediate reward, almost all animals, especially humans, perform many activities so that in the future they, their family, friends, and colleagues can survive and be rewarded or not be hurt, injured, or killed.

There are several systems that activate our motor system. For example, if some object causes pain we will move away from this painful object. If we get too cold, we look for something that will warm us, and if our body temperature gets too high, we look for some means to cool off. We have networks in our body and brain that audit our metabolism. Therefore, if we get dehydrated, we get thirsty and look for something to drink. If our blood sugar drops, we get hungry and we look for food and eat. When our bladders are full or we have to have a bowel movement, we look for a bathroom and empty our bladder or rectum. If we need more oxygen, we breathe more rapidly and deeply. These are all called homeostatic mechanisms.

We also know about emotions that will be discussed below, if we feel emotions such as fear, disgust, or some forms of sadness, we will want to move away-escape. If we feel happiness or anger, we might want to approach.

Throughout our lives, we learn the conditions that are likely to help us experience positive emotions, and the conditions that are most likely to produce negative emotions. We also learn some of the best means for obtaining the items that we will need. Most of this information is stored in our brain as declarative memories. Although new declarative memories are stored in our brains by the previously described Papez circuit, this knowledge, for the most part, is stored in the sensory association areas and polymodal sensory association area found in the temporal and posterior parietal lobes.

The frontal lobes are strongly connected to these stored memories with large cables that travel under our cerebral cortex and these cables are called longitudinal fasciculi. In addition, the frontal lobes are strongly connected with critical areas that mediate emotion such as the amygdala, the reward circuits in the ventral striatum with the nucleus accumbens, and the hypothalamus, which monitors our internal milieu. Since the prefrontal lobes receive all this information, it can make computations about what will be or might be needed in the future. The prefrontal lobes are also connected with the premotor cortex and thus this connectivity allows this frontal lobe to initiate goal-oriented activities, have us persist until our goals are accomplished, and terminate these activities if they cannot be accomplished.

The history of Phineas Gage is one of the most famous stories about the frontal lobes. In 1868, John Harlow wrote about this very hard-working supervisor. To clear the way for railroad tracks, explosives had to be placed into rocks. While Gage was placing explosives with an iron tamping bar, there was an explosion and this explosion sent this bar flying at high speeds. This bar entered Gage's skull on one side and then came out on the other side, destroying his frontal lobes. It was amazing that this did not kill him, but he not only did survive but was also able to speak normally and use all his limbs. However, this injury caused a traumatic frontal lobectomy. After this episode, it was reported that he had a dramatic change in his personality. Before this accident, Harlow stated that Gage "was energetic and persistent in executing his plans." However, according to Harlow, after this accident, he failed to carry out his plans. His personality was so changed that his friends and family said, "He was no longer Gage."

There are several elements to successfully initiating, executing, and completing plans. In order to live a full, meaningful life, a person has to self-initiate activities and patients with frontal lobe dysfunction are impaired at the self-initiation of actions. When they are hungry they will look for food, when they are thirsty they will look for something to drink, when they get hot they will turn on the air conditioner, and if they get cold they will turn on their heater. However, it is unlikely they will go shopping for food if not hungry, or pay their electric bill, clean their house, or even go to work. This self-motivation disorder is called abulia.

In order to successfully initiate a new goal-oriented activity, the first step is discontinuing a former behavior. Denny-Brown (1958), who worked closely with many patients who had a brain injury and disease, reported that patients with injury to their frontal lobes often had abnormal approach motor behaviors and were impaired at disengaging. For example, when I was a neurology resident during Grand Rounds at the Harvard Neurological Unit, Dr. Denny-Brown asked a patient with a frontal injury to open their hands and to keep their hands relaxed on their lap with their palms up. Denny-Brown then placed his index finger in the palm of this patient's hand and as Denny-Brown expected, this patient grasped his finger. After Denny-Brown removed his finger and told the patient to just keep his hand relaxed, when Denny-Brown again touched his hand this patient again grasped his finger. This abnormal behavior is called the grasp reflex. Denny-Brown also noted that when he was moving his hands in front of this patient with a frontal lobe disease, even without touching the patient's hand, the patient would often reach out and grasp his hand. Denny-Brown called this "magnetic apraxia." Lhermitte (1983), a French neurologist, noted that when patients with frontal injuries were seated at a table and there was an object on the table that could be used, with being asked, and without a need to use that which was on the table, they would still use it. For example, even when not thirsty, when there was a pitcher of water and an empty glass on the table, the patient with frontal injury would pick up the pitcher, fill the glass with water, and then drink some of this water. Lhermitte called this "utilization behavior."

We also developed a clinical test we call "crossed response inhibition." We ask patients to put their hands on their laps, palm down, and when we touch their left hand, they are to lift their right hand and when we touch their right hand, they are to lift their left hand. We also ask them to do this as rapidly as possible. Patients with frontal lobe dysfunction will often lift the hand that was touched, rather than the opposite hand. A similar test can be performed with the eyes, such that the examiner puts their left hand on the right side of the patient's head and their right hand to the left of the patient's head and eyes. The examiner then tells the patient, "When I move the hand on your right side, you look at the hand on the opposite side and vice versa." Patients with frontal lobe injury will often incorrectly look at the moving hand.

All these disorders have a similar basic mechanism, a failure to disengage from stimuli. This ability to disengage from a useless activity is often needed to initiate a goal-oriented activity and there are also some patients who can initially disengage, but some people with frontal dysfunction, even after they get started, can get stuck and repeatedly as well as incorrectly perform the same action over and over again. This getting stuck and not going forward in the midst of activity is called perseveration. In the clinic, we perform a very simple test for perseveration. We ask our patients to write in script the letters m and n as well as to alternate writing these two letters. Patients with frontal dysfunction, however, will often start to perseverate and then just continue to write one of these two letters (e.g., mnmnmnmmmmmmmmmmmmmm).

The disengagement failures from frontal lobe dysfunction are not limited to movements as mentioned earlier. These disengagement failures can even influence these patients' thinking. One of the tests psychologists use to test frontal lobe dysfunction is called Stroop Test. In this test, patients are provided with a list of words that name different colors, such as blue, red, green, and yellow. Some of these words are printed in colors of ink that are different from the words they spell. For example, the word blue can be printed with red ink and the word red with green ink. The person taking this test is asked to name the colored print and not read the word, and to name these colors as rapidly as possible. Patients with frontal dysfunction will often read the word rather than name the color of the ink because they are impaired at disengagement.

In order to move forward, not only does a person have to disengage, initiate an activity, alter the activity as needed, but they also must continue performing this activity until the job is completed. Patients with frontal lobe dysfunction often fail to complete a project because in addition to disorders of initiation, and failures of disengagement with perseveration, they also often have a failure to persist at performing activities until they have been completed. This disorder is called impersistence. In clinic, we do a simple test for impersistence. We ask our patients to close their eyes, open their mouth, and stick out their tongue until we tell them the task is complete. Many patients with frontal lobe dysfunction will open their eyes or close their mouth after a few seconds, but this test will only detect those people with the most severe forms of impersistence. Many patients with frontal lobe dysfunction are also easily distracted and an increase of distractibility can also cause impersistence.

To survive, be successful, and have a full life, we must go forward, and to go forward in a new direction, we need to disengage, initiate a new activity, not perseverate, and persist until successful.

Emotional Actions

Emotional experiences often determine if we approach or stay or if we go-avoid. Wilhelm Wundt (1832–1920) was a physician, who many credit with being one of the founders of modern psychology. In 1903, Wundt presented one of the first analyses of emotions. He proposed that emotional experiences vary in three dimensions: quality (good or bad), excitement (arousal), and activity. About one-half century later, Osgood, Suci, and Tanenbaum (1957) had normal subjects verbally assess emotions and then performed a factor analysis on these judgments. Osgood et al., like Wundt, assumed that emotion can be defined as a coincidence of values. However, rather than activity these investigators found that the third factor was dominance (in control/out of control). Brandley and Lang (1994) developed a non-verbal pictorial assessment technique that directly measures pleasure–displeasure (valence), arousal, and dominance associated with a person's affective reaction to a wide variety of stimuli. The Self-Assessment Manikin (SAM) is a nonverbal pic-torial assessment technique that measures these three components of an emotion by having the participant point that one manikin from a series of manikins that best represent an emotion. The three components assessed on this manikin are valence (sad face to a smiling face), arousal (small beats of the heart represented by small stars) to large beats (represented by large stars), and control (represented by small manikins to large manikins).

Frijda (2016), however, also explored the cognitive structure of emotion and found, as Wundt posited, that action readiness, instead of control, should be the third factor. On the basis of this dimensional view of emotions, Heilman (1997) suggested that the conscious experience of emotion may be mediated by three anatomically distributed modular networks, including one that determines quality or valence (positive to negative), a second network that controls the level of arousal (high to low), and a third network that mediates motor activation. This motor activation can be directed toward the stimulus that induced this emotion (approach) or directed away from the stimulus (avoid) or neutral (no action needed). Figure 3.2 illustrates this revised manikin with three rows: valence, arousal, and motor activation.

Valence

In regard to valence, we have already mentioned the reports that have described that with left hemisphere injury, patients often appear to be depressed and after right hemispheric injury, patients often are indifferent or inappropriately euphoric. In addition to this clinical data, several functional imaging studies performed on patients with depression suggested that left hemisphere appears to be hypoactive (Bench et al., 1992; Phelps et al., 1984). In addition, by using electrophysiological techniques, Davidson et al. (1979) and Tucker (1981) demonstrated in normal subjects that whereas the left hemisphere mediates emotions with positive valence, the right hemisphere mediates emotions with negative valence. The mechanism by which each hemisphere mediates positive and negative valence is unknown. There are however some hemispheric asymmetries that are in concert with this positive–negative valence, left–right hemispheric dichotomy. As will be discussed, several emotions are associated with high levels of arousal such as anger and fear. Studies of patients with stroke have revealed that patients with a right hemisphere stroke often reveal a decreased level of arousal, and those with left hemisphere strokes reveal an

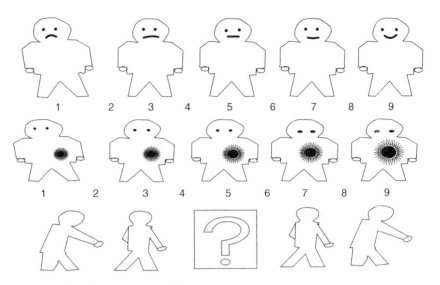

FIGURE 3.2 Self-Assessment Manikin

After participants are shown pictures that are designed to elicit different emotions, they are then asked to mark the manikin that represents the valence of the emotion (top row) they experienced and then how aroused the stimulus made them feel (middle row). The third row is called "dominance." However, we have altered this to avoidance (small figure on the left side of the third row, or approach, that are the figures on the right side of the third row).

increase in arousal (Heilman et al., 1978). In addition, some emotions are associated with increased activity of the sympathetic nervous system, which prepares the body for fight or flight and the sympathetic system is primary controlled by the right hemisphere.

The amygdala, a portion of the limbic system, is critical in mediating emotions such as fear and anger. The activity of the amygdala is controlled by its connections to other parts of the brain such as the frontal lobes (Figure 3.3) and there appear to be asymmetries in the connectivity between the cortex of the left and right hemisphere with the left and right amygdala (Baker & Kim, 2004). This asymmetry may also play an important factor in valence and why there are hemispheric asymmetries in mediating emotions with positive and negative valence.

Since the time of Hippocrates, it has been postulated that body humors can influence mood. Tucker and Williamson (1984) suggested that hemispheric valence asymmetries might be related to asymmetrical control of neurotransmitters. This hypothesis was supported by a functional imaging study using positron emission tomography (PET) imaging. Robinson and Starkstein (1989) reported that after left hemisphere stroke there was reduced serotonergic receptor binding and that after a right hemisphere stroke there was increased serotonergic binding. They also found that the lower the serotonergic binding, the worse the depression. Psychiatrists often treat people with depression by giving medications that increase the activity

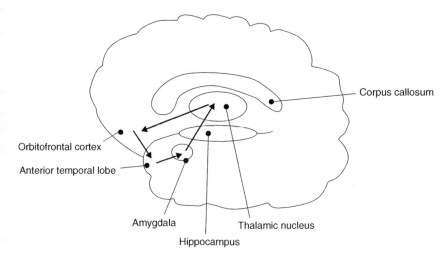

FIGURE 3.3 Connections between the Frontal Lobes and the Amygdala—The Basolateral Limbic Circuit

The amygdala is the part of the limbic system that is critical in the mediation of emotional feelings and behaviors, especially fear and anger. The activity of the amygdala is in part controlled by the orbital (lower) portion of the frontal lobes. In this basolateral limbic circuit (also called Yakovlev's circuit, after the person who first described this circuit), the orbital frontal cortex in each hemisphere is connected with the anterior portion of the temporal lobe of each hemisphere and this portion of the temporal lobes connects with the amygdala. The amygdala projects to the thalamus (deep in each hemisphere) and the thalamus projects back to the orbitofrontal cortex.

Removal of the anterior temporal lobes in animals was first performed by Kluver and Bucy and the disorder it causes is now called the Kluver–Bucy syndrome. The animals and people who have this disorder do not show fear or anger because the basolateral (Yakovlev's) circuit is destroyed. They also show other problems because other areas are injured, for example, impaired memory, because the hippocampus is injured, and visual object agnosia, because the ventral visual association cortex (the "what" stream) may also be injured.

of this serotonergic system. Although clinical psychiatry has provided strong evidence that depression is associated with a reduction of serotonin, it remains unclear how these differences in neurotransmitters induce emotions with a positive and negative valence.

Arousal

Certain mental states are often difficult to define, and arousal is one of them. An aroused person, however, is awake, alert, and has a brain that is prepared to process incoming stimuli and perform actions. In contrast, an unaroused person is lethargic, sleepy, or comatose and is not prepared to process stimuli or perform actions.

Outside the central nervous system, arousal usually refers to activation of the sympathetic nervous system that causes the pupils in the eyes to dilate, the hands to sweat, and the heart rate to beat more rapidly.

In the central nervous system, arousal refers to the excitatory state of neurons or the propensity of neurons to discharge when appropriately activated. Active neurons need more energy than inactive neurons and this energy requires fuel (glucose) and oxygen. Glucose and oxygen are brought to the brain by blood, and therefore, the portions of the brain that are more active are supplied with more blood. Functional imaging such as with PET or fMRI measures the changes in blood flow. Arousal-activation of different portions of the brain is usually measured by increase in blood flow. Therefore, these imaging methods can help reveal the areas of the brain that are focally active-aroused.

Arousal can also be measured physiologically with electroencephalography (EEG). When the brain gets aroused, the waves seen on the EEG get more rapid with a lower amplitude and this is called desynchronization.

In addition, to the focal arousal of specific parts of the brain, during the time a specific area is performing its specialized activity, brain arousal can be more general. Arousal and attention are closely linked and arousal appears to be mediated by a cortical–limbic–reticular network (Heilman, 1979; Watson et al., 1981; Mesulam, 1981). Arousal of each hemisphere is controlled by an area in the midbrain and thalamus called the reticular activating system. In one of the most important neuro-physiology studies, Moruzzi and Magoun (1949) demonstrated that stimulation of the reticular formation, in animals, induces both behavioral and physiological arousal. Bilateral lesions of this reticular formation induce coma. A unilateral lesion causes a decrease of arousal in the ipsilateral hemisphere (Watson et al., 1974) such that this hemisphere goes into a state of coma. This reticular activating system is partially controlled by certain areas of the cortex. For example, studies have revealed that stimulation of certain cortical areas can alter arousal. Stimulation of polymodal and supramodal cortices, such as the prefrontal lobe or the inferior parietal lobe, increases arousal by activating the mesencephalic reticular formation (Segundo et al., 1955). The areas are critical for mediating attention, action-intention, and cognition. Therefore, control of arousal would be an important additional function.

Although, for the most part, an aroused-alert person can perform almost all activities better than an unaroused person, when arousal get very high, it may inter-fere with some of the brain's functions. In 1908, Yerkes and Dodson noted that as arousal increased, performance improved, but that in this relationship there was a peak of arousal level and after this peak was reached, further arousal causes a deterioration of performance. The relationship between arousal and performance is often illustrated with a bell-shaped curve with arousal on the horizontal axis and performance on the vertical axis. For example, it has known for many years that there are people who when taking an examination become very anxious, and thus perform poorly on tests. When they are given a medication that helps to reduce their anxiety associated with high level of arousal, their performance is dramatic-ally improved. It has also been noted that there is a relationship between creativity and arousal. Many of the most creative advances have been associated with lower states of arousal. For example, Isaac Newton was sitting under an apple tree on his mother's farm when he developed the law of gravity. Gregor Mendel was taking care of his garden when he developed the laws of genetics and even Charles Darwin was on a cruise when he developed the theory of evolution.

Sensory information coming into brain is transmitted through the nuclei deep in each hemisphere called the thalamus (Figure 1.6). The thalamus is almost like the checkpoint at the border of a country where government agents decide who will enter and who will not enter the country. The stimuli that thalamus allow to enter are transmitted to the cerebral cortex. The information coming from the thalamus is sent to primary sensory cortices of the cerebral cortex. The visual primary cortex is in the occipital lobe, the somatosensory (touch, hot–cold, limb movement) cortex is at the front portion of the parietal cortex, and the primary auditory cortex is on the top of the superior temporal lobe (Figure 3.4). Each of these primary sensory cortical areas performs an elemental analysis of the incoming information. For example, the primary auditory cortex analyzes the pitch, amplitude, and duration

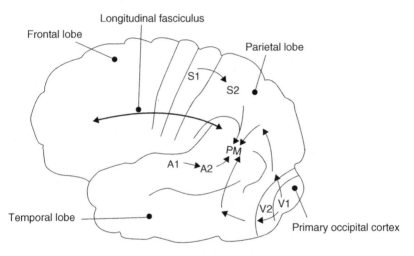

FIGURE 3.4 Primary Sensory Cortical Areas of Vision, Hearing, Touching-Feeling, Their Association Areas, and Polymodal Areas

The primary somatosensory cortex (S1), which is at the front portion of the parietal lobe, is connected with its association cortex (S2) in the more posterior superior parietal lobe. Similarly, the primary auditory cortex (A!), which is on the top mid-portion of the temporal lobe, is connected to its association cortex (A2). The primary visual cortex (V1) is also connected to its association cortex (V2) and then, as illustrated in Figures 2.3–2.5, divides in a ventral stream important for object recognition (what) and a dorsal stream important in determining object location. All these areas of sensory association cortex then send projects to the inferior parietal lobe called polymodal cortex (PM). This polymodal cortex connects with the prefrontal lobe by a white matter pathway called the longitudinal fasciculus.

of sounds. After these fundamental analyses, each sensory cortex sends this information to its specific (unimodal) sensory association cortex. These modality specific sensory association areas are adjacent to each of the primary sensory cortices. These primary cortical association areas store sensory-specific information, which allows us to be able to perceive these stimuli. Patients with injury to these association cortical areas can still detect incoming stimuli, but they cannot perceive these stimuli. Thus, depending on the area damaged, they do not know what they are seeing, hearing, or feeling. For example, when people have a deficit in their visual association cortex, they can have a deficit called visual agnosia. Not only will they be unable to recognize objects, but also even when they are looking at a simple design, such as a drawing of a clock face, they do not know what they are looking at and they cannot even copy this drawing.

After incoming stimuli are analyzed by their specific association (i.e., visual, auditory, and somesthetic) areas (Figure 3.4), they meet, congregate, and interact in what is called polymodal and supramodal areas, such as the inferior parietal lobe. It is in these polymodal and supramodal areas of the brain, such as the inferior parietal lobe, where objects are recognized.

Supramodal cortical areas, such as the inferior parietal lobe, also receive and send information to the frontal lobes. This information is important in determining goal-oriented behaviors. This supramodal area also receives and sends information to the limbic system by the cingulate gyrus. This information is important for the interaction between object knowledge, goals, and emotions. This knowledge allows us to determine the significance of what we are viewing, hearing, or touching.

The significance of a stimulus requires knowledge as to both the meaning of the stimulus and our motivational state. Our motivational state is determined by many factors, but the three most important factors include: (1) our immediate biological needs, such as hunger and thirst; (2) our emotions; and (3) our long-term goals. Our internal milieu is monitored by portions of the limbic system together with the hypothalamus. Therefore, limbic input into regions important in determining stimulus significance may provide information about immediate biological needs. In addition, the information about long-term goals, not motivated by immediate biological needs, is provided by the frontal lobes (Stuss & Benson, 1986). As mentioned, the frontal lobes are the part of the cerebral cortex where there is also a convergence of information, including perceived stimuli from the sensory association areas and semantic knowledge stored in the posterior polymodal regions such as the inferior parietal.

Changes in the level of arousal in the central nervous system are usually associated with changes in the activity of the peripheral autonomic nervous system. One means of measuring the activity of the autonomic nervous system is to measure hand sweating (e.g., galvanic skin response). We measured (Heilman et al., 1978) the galvanic skin response in the hand, in response to an uncomfortable but not painful electronic shock of patients who had right or left hemispheric strokes, as well as healthy control participants. We found that patients with a right hemisphere lesion had a reduced galvanic skin response. Other investigators have reported similar findings (Schrandt et al., 1989). There was an additional finding that we reported in this chapter.

We also found that when compared to the healthy participants, the patients with left hemisphere lesions appear to have a greater autonomic response (Heilman et al., 1978). Subsequently, in another study, Yokoyama et al. (1987) measured changes in heart rate, as a measure of arousal, and they found similar results. Using PET, Perani et al. (1993) also found metabolic depression of the left hemisphere in cases of right hemisphere stroke.

The brain mechanism that could account for this asymmetrical hemispheric control of arousal remains unknown. Like many other asymmetries, it may be related to connectivity with the right hemisphere having privileged communication with both sides of the reticular activating system.

Motor Activation

As mentioned, the dimensional view of emotions (Heilman, 1997) suggests that the conscious experience of emotion may be mediated by three anatomically distributed modular networks. The valence and arousal networks have been discussed and this section describes the motor activation network.

There are several emotions that call for action. In general, we, like other animals, would like to avoid stimuli that induce unpleasant emotions and approach stimuli that induce pleasant emotions. However, valence (positive versus negative) does not fully account for the stimuli we approach and avoid. For example, anger is an emotion with high negative valence and high arousal, yet the action often associated with anger is approach.

Meaningful goal-oriented motor actions are performed by a motor network that includes the motor cortex, the corticospinal track, the lower motor neurons, and muscles (Figures 3.1 and 3.2). Injury to any portion of this motor system may cause weakness. However, the network that is important in initiating these movements is called the action-intentional network. This network is a modular network that includes portions of the cerebral cortex, basal ganglia, and limbic system. In humans and other primates, the dorsolateral frontal lobes along with the basal ganglia appear to be the fulcrum of this motor preparatory network. Patients with injury to this intentional network have deficits that may appear to be a form of weakness, but in these patients their motor network, including their motor cortex, corticospinal track, motor neurons, and muscles, is all intact. However, patients who have impairments of their action–intentional networks may fail to initiate actions because their intact motor neurons in the motor cortex are not activated and do not fire (Watson et al.., 1978). For example, humans and monkeys with a unilateral frontal lesion may show evidence of the hemispatial neglect syndrome. Patients with the unilateral neglect syndrome often fail to respond to stimuli in the space that is contralateral to their brain injury. In addition, they may also fail to make movements toward this side of space. This failure to move in one direction can be seen with the eyes, head–neck, and upper limbs. For example, if coins are placed on a table in front of these patients, on both sides of the patients' midline, the patients are blindfolded and are asked to pick up all these coins, patients with neglect will often fail to pick up the coins on the side opposite to their brain injury. It was thought that this disorder was being caused by visual inattention-unawareness such that they did not pick up these coins because they were unaware of their presence. However, it is possible that these patients have an action-intentional disorder with an impairment in moving to or in the space opposite their brain lesion.

Most commonly, unilateral spatial neglect is caused by a stroke that injures the right parietal lobe and these patients are inattentive to, and unaware of, the objects in the space that is to the left side of their body. However, unilateral spatial neglect can also occur with injury to frontal lobes. To learn if frontal injuries cause unilateral spatial neglect because of spatial inattention (unawareness) or a failure to act in this portion of space, we performed an experiment where monkeys were trained to respond with their left hand when stimulated on their right side, and to respond with their right hand when stimulated on their left side. We then removed a portion of their frontal lobe on one side. After we did this surgery, the animals appeared to neglect stimuli on the side opposite of this surgery. However, after this injury (e.g., the right frontal lobe), when the side opposite their injury (e.g., left side) was stimulated, they correctly moved their arm on the side of the injury (e.g., right side). In contrast, when stimulated on the side of their lesion (e.g., right side), they failed to move the arm on the opposite side (e.g., left side). However, these monkeys were not weak. These results suggested that frontal lobe dysfunction can cause a form of spatial action-intentional disorder, rather than a disorder of sensory inattention. After we learned about this in monkeys, we have found similar deficits in humans, where there are impairments in moving in one direction, acting in one-half of space, and even failure to move the limbs on one side of the body. In humans, frontal neglect with these forms of akinesia is more frequently associated with right than left hemisphere injury.

Further evidence of the importance of the dorsolateral frontal lobes comes from physiological studies where investigators (Goldberg & Bushnell 1981) recorded from cells in the dorsolateral frontal lobe. This study revealed that neurons in the frontal lobe have enhanced activity when the animal is presented with a stimulus that is meaningful and predicts movement.

The reason the dorsolateral frontal lobes are important in the initiation of actions is again related to their connectivity. The dorsolateral frontal lobes receive input from multimodal and supramodal posterior cortical sensory association areas, such as the inferior parietal lobe. The input from these areas provides the frontal lobes with information about the stimuli, being seen, heard, or felt. The frontal lobes are also strongly connected with the cingulate gyrus and the cingulate gyrus receives information from portions of the emotional limbic system, and this emotional information from the limbic systems is an important factor in motivation for action. Finally, the dorsolateral frontal lobes participate in a cortical–basal ganglia–thalamo–cortical loop (Alexander, DeLong, & Strick 1986). This network is important in activating the premotor areas in the frontal lobes and it is these premotor areas that activate the motor cortex.

The concepts that the frontal lobes are important in goal-oriented actions and also rejection behaviors may seem to be contradictory, but in order to perform goal-oriented behaviors a person had to disengage from performing meaningless actions on meaningless stimuli and instead initiate actions that are important for meaningful goal-oriented activities. Typically, patients with frontal lobe dysfunction are impaired at both disengaging from meaningless stimuli and initiating actions for meaningful goal-oriented activities.

Whereas the frontal lobes appear to be important in the initiation of meaningful actions, it remains unclear if there are different networks that mediate approach versus avoidance behaviors. Denny-Brown and Chambers (1958), however, noted that every animal has two basic forms of behavior, approach, and avoidance. They posited that whereas the posterior temporal and parietal lobes were important in approach behaviors, the frontal lobes were important in avoidance behaviors such as disengagement. At first this sounds like it would be contradictory to the postulate discussed earlier that the frontal lobes are critical for goal-oriented behaviors. However, to test this hypothesis, Denny-Brown and Chambers performed surgery on monkeys, removing their right and left parietal lobes. After this surgery, they noted that these monkeys' behavior was characterized by strong withdrawal from several forms of stimulation, for example, avoiding being touched on their limbs or head. Denny-Brown called this disorder repellant apraxia.

A similar withdrawal-avoidance has been reported by Mori and Yamadori (1989) in four human patients who had bilateral parietal lesions. When these patients were touched on the limbs or head, they responded with exaggerated withdrawal movements and refused to be touched on the lips and tongue. These behavioral changes resulted in difficulty in eating. These touches were not painful to these patients. These behavioral alterations can be interpreted as a rejection of contact. We call these actions "avoidance behaviors"; however, these authors called this disorder "rejection behavior."

Overall, these studies suggest that whereas the frontal lobes are important in performing goal-oriented activities, the parietal lobes are important in engagement and the frontal lobes disengagement.

In our Memory Disorders Clinics, we see patients with two common forms of dementing diseases where behaviors appear to be in accordance with the frontal disengagement and parietal engagement hypotheses.

We often see patients in our clinics who appear to have early Alzheimer's disease. When a new patient comes into my office, the first thing I do is welcome them and have a conversation with them. I often ask them where they come from and why they came to see me. These patients often turn to their significant other, so that the person accompanying them could answer these and many other questions that I ask. I first thought, with this disease, they most likely lost their memory and could not recall the answers to these simple questions. But then I thought maybe they do know the answer to my questions, but they do not want to interact with me (rejection of contact or avoidance behavior). To learn if this may be the case, with several patients, after they turned to their significant other so that they could answer my questions, I said to them, "Please do try and answer my questions." I found that they often knew the answers to the questions that I asked them.

When I spoke to these patient's significant others about their social behavior, I was often told that there had been a dramatic reduction of initiating social interactions, even when their living conditions had not changed. When I asked why, I was often told, well they no longer like to spend time with friends. For example, one husband told me that his wife loved to go out on Friday evenings, meet friends at a restaurant, have a drink or two before dinner, and then have dinner with these friends, but now she never wants to do this. The husband, who was her caregiver, told me that he thought this isolation was related to her wife's disabilities and being embarrassed about her cognitive and memory loss. However, when I ask these patients why they are seeing me, they often responded, "Well my husband brought me here." When I asked why their husband, or wife, or caregiver brought them to clinic, they often did not know. When I asked them about their memory, most were unaware that they had a memory problem or other cognitive disorders. Many of these patients with Alzheimer's disease have what is called "anosognosia." This word comes from three units: 'a' = without, 'noso' = disease, and 'gnosia' = knowledge. Therefore, it is unlikely that these patients become socially isolated because they are embarrassed about their disability.

Most commonly, patients with Alzheimer's disease first develop problems with their episodic memory. Therefore, after we give these patients three words for them to remember, we ask them other questions about their orientation (day of the week, the month and day of the month, the year, and their current location) and then we ask them about the words they were asked to remember. Patients with Alzheimer's often cannot recall these words. When their brain is imaged, by using MRI, their brain images show that a part of the brain, called the hippocampus, has atrophied. However, as the disease progresses, the next areas to reveal degeneration are the posterior parietal lobes. These areas are important for naming, calculating, performing learned skilled movements, knowing the name of fingers, and recalling directions. These disorders are caused by degeneration of their parietal lobes. Like those patients who had strokes of their parietal lobes, who were discussed earlier, these patients might have changes in their social interactions because with their parietal lobe degeneration, they reveal avoidance behaviors.

In 2006, Uc et al. published an article that support hypothesis about the relationship between Alzheimer's disease and avoidance. These investigators noticed that drivers with cognitive impairment are more likely to get into vehicular accidents and that rear-end collisions are the most common types of accidents. They tested avoidance in 61 drivers with mild Alzheimer's disease and 115 elderly controls using a driving simulator. After a segment of uneventful driving, each driver suddenly encountered a vehicle in front of them that stopped at an intersection, creating the potential for a collision with the lead vehicle. A large percent age of the drivers with Alzheimer's had unsafe outcomes. Many of these participants revealed risky avoidance behavior, such as slowing down abruptly or prematurely, or swerving out of the traffic lane. For example, 70% of drivers with Alzheimer's disease slowed down abruptly versus 37% of elderly controls and abrupt slowing increased the odds of being struck from behind by another vehicle.

But how does avoidance behavior influence emotions? We (Drago et al., 2010) studied patients with Alzheimer's disease to learn how this disease may influence emotional experiences. Our results revealed that when participants with Alzheimer's disease are asked to assess the emotional valence of pictures that normally induce emotions (The International Affective Picture System), they judged the pictures that portray pleasant scenes as less pleasant than did the controls. When they viewed unpleasant pictures, they rated these as less unpleasant than did the controls. These results suggest that patients with Alzheimer's disease do have a reduction in the intensity of their emotional experiences and/or responses to seeing emotional scenes.

Some patients with Alzheimer's disease can have some depression, and depression can be associated with a reduced emotional response; however, the participants with Alzheimer's disease, who participated in this study, were assessed and not found to be depressed. Further, patients with depression have a stronger response to negative than positive pictures, but in this study, the patients with Alzheimer's disease showed no greater response to negative than positive stimuli. Patients with Alzheimer's disease can also have visuospatial disorders that might impair their ability to recognize the emotions being portrayed in these pictures. However, if these participants with Alzheimer's disease had a sufficient degradation of the systems that mediate visual perception or if they could not comprehend these pictures, these participants with Alzheimer's disease should be impaired recognizing objects on this picture naming test. Although rarely, patients with Alzheimer's disease can have a visual agnosia, when these patients were assessed with the Boston Naming Test, and they had no evidence of not being able to comprehend the meaning of pictures on this test.

Emotional experiences and the knowledge of what future conditions may induce emotions are the major sources of motivation for many activities. The results of this study by Drago et al. suggest that there appears to be a reduction of both positive and negative emotions and this reduction may be related to a failure of engagement, and this failure may be related to the degeneration of their parietal lobes. However, there are alternative explanations. For example, studies of patients with Alzheimer's disease have suggested that even at the earliest stages of this disease there is a neuronal deterioration of the amygdala (Silvio Ramos Bernardes da Silva Filho et al., 2017) and it has been well established that the amygdala is critical for experiencing emotions, especially those with negative valence. Fear conditioning (a research method where animals and humans learn to fear certain stimuli) is strongly dependent on amygdala functioning, and research has revealed that it is impaired in patients with Alzheimer's disease (Hamann et al., 2002). In addition, a functional neuroimaging study investigated the common areas of activations when healthy people are exposed to facial expressions of emotion and emotionally evocative scenes and both these sets of stimuli activate the amygdala.

Patients with Alzheimer's disease also often have degeneration of the nucleus of Meynert, a critical element of the cholinergic network as well as the locus coeruleus, an important systems for providing the brain with norepinephrine. This neurotransmitter is important for arousal and as discussed arousal is a critical element in emotional experience. Therefore, perhaps in patients with Alzheimer's disease, it is the degeneration of these portions of the arousal network that accounted for their reduced valence ratings.

Future research is needed to learn if failure of people with Alzheimer's disease to fully experience emotion is related to faulty engagement, deterioration of their limbic system, or alterations of arousal.

Introversion–Extraversion

Merriam-Webster defines an introvert as a person whose attention and interests are directed toward their own thoughts and feelings. In contrast, an extrovert is a person whose interests and attention are directed outward. In the prior section, we discussed that according to Denny-Brown and Chambers (1958), the prefrontal portion of the frontal lobes is important for disengagement and the posterior parietal and temporal lobes for engagement.

Forsman et al. (2012) noted that extraversion appears to be dependent on two sets of neural circuitries—an activating system that induces approach behaviors and an inhibitory system that mediates avoidance behaviors. According to the authors, extraversion is due to a strong activating system and a weak inhibitory system. In contrast, introversion is related to a weak activating system and a strong inhibitory system. Forsman et al. reviewed several studies that found extraversion to be negatively related to cortical thickness in frontal regions in young adults (Wright et al., 2006; Barrós-Loscertales et al., 2006). This may help to explain why patients with early Alzheimer's disease with parietal degeneration appear to be introverted.

CONCLUSION

While we are awake, there are two major means by which our brain can be engaged, externally and internally. When our brain is engaged externally, we are most often interacting with something or someone in our environment that we see, hear, feel, smell, or taste. We not only attend to these stimuli but also perform actions that allow us to interact with these stimuli.

In contrast, when we are internally engaged, we are often attending inward, hearing words we are speaking to ourselves, seeing all different kinds of images, and hearing people speaking, music, and sounds.

One day I was home sitting on our couch, thinking about something that had happened to me many years ago. When I was about ten years old, my mother needed to go to work and she was worried that when I came home from school there would be no one in our apartment to greet me. I wanted to have a dog greet me. However, the owners of our apartment said we were not allowed to have dogs. My mother thought we could buy a bird, a parakeet, and this bird could keep me company when I came home from school. We bought a beautiful blue parakeet, who I named "Chirpy." This tiny bird became a loving little friend. Each day when I came home from school, I would open his cage, and he would fly around our house and land on my shoulder. Before letting Chirpy out of his cage, I would usually check all the windows in our apartment to make certain they were all closed so that he could not fly out of an open window. But one day I let him out, there was an open window, and he flew out. I opened the window and yelled "Chirpy! Please come back." I even opened all the other windows in our apartment so that he could find his way home. But I never did see him again.

While I was just sitting on the couch thinking about my Chirpy, my father came home from work, came into the living room where I was sitting, and said, "Why are you looking so sad?"

DOI: 10.4324/9781003206682-5

I told him, "Chirpy flew out of the window. I was just thinking about Chirpy. I already miss him."

My father told me, "You should always look forward, and not look back. Looking back makes people sad."

It takes me a long time to get some things done. About 70 years after my father gave me this advice, we did a study about looking back (Williamson et al., 2019). I had thought that based on the possible survival value of our memories of negative events, the recall of negative emotional memories would be more important for our survival and well-being than the memories of positive emotional events. We, therefore, posited that when given an open-ended request to recall either a sad or a happy memory, people are more likely to recall an older sad memory than a happy one. We asked healthy participants from the age group of 18 to 63 years to freely recall happy and sad emotional memories and estimate the length of time that had passed since the recalled event had occurred. We then analyzed the age of each memory based on valence. We found that our participants significantly volunteered more remote sad than happy memories. Further, these participants' sad memories were more remote than their happy memories. Yes, I still think about my Chirpy and it still makes me sad. Although this does not entirely prove my father's advice, it certainly supports his postulate. Please "look forward."

REFERENCES

Acosta LM, Bennett JA, and Heilman KM. (2014). Callosal disconnection and limb-kinetic apraxia. *Neurocase.* 20(6):599–605.

Akelaitis AJ. (1945). Studies on the corpus callosum IV. Diagonistic dyspraxia in epileptics following partial and complete section of the corpus callosum. *Am J Psychiatry.* 101:594–9.

Alexander GE, DeLong MR, and Strick PL. (1986). Parallel organization of functionally segregated circuits linking basal ganglia and cortex. *Annu Rev Neurosci.* 9:357–81.

Annett, M. (1998). Handedness and cerebral dominance: the right shift theory. *J Neuropsychiatry Clin Neurosci.* Fall; 10(4):459–69.

Babinski J. (1914). Contribution à l'etude des troubles mentaux dans l'hémiplégie organique cérébrale (anosognosie). *Revue Neurologique.* 27:845–7.

Baker KB and Kim JJ. (2004). Amygdala lateralization in fear conditioning: evidence for greater involvement of the right amygdala. *Behav Neurosci.* Feb; 118(1):15–23.

Bálint R. (1909). Seelenlähmung des "Schauens," optische Ataxie, räumliche Störung der Aufmerksamkeit. *Monatschr Psychiat Neurol.* 25:51–81.

Barrós-Loscertales A, Meseguer V, Sanjuán A, Belloch V, Parcet MA, Torrubia R, and Avila C. (2006). Striatum gray matter reduction in males with an overactive behavioral activation system. *Eur J Neurosci.* Oct; 24(7):2071–4.

Bench CJ, Friston KJ, Brown RG, Scott LC, Frackowiak RS, and Dolan RJ. (1992). The anatomy of melancholia—focal abnormalities of cerebral blood flow in major depression. *Psychol Med.* Aug; 22(3):607–15.

Berthier M, Starkstein S, and Leiguarda R. (1987). Behavioral effects of damage to the right insula and surrounding regions. *Cortex.* Dec; 23(4):673–8.

Bowers D and Heilman K. (1980). Pseudoneglect: effects of hemispace on a tactile line bisection. *Neuropsychologia.* 18:491–8.

Bradley MM and Lang PJ. (1994). Measuring emotion: the Self-Assessment Manikin and the Semantic Differential. *Lang Behav Ther Exp Psychiatry.* 25(1): 49–59.

Broca P. (1861). Remarques sur le siege de la faculte du language articule, suivies d'une observation d'aphemie. *Bull Soc Anat, Paris.* 2:330–57.

Broca P. (1865). Sur le siège de la faculté du langage articulé (15 juin). *Bulletins de la Société d'Anthropologie de Paris.* 6:377–93.

Bruder, GE, Stewart JW, and McGrath PJ. (2007). Right brain, left brain in depressive disorders: clinical and theoretical implications of behavioral, electrophysiological and neuroimaging findings. *Neurosci Biobehav Rev.* Jul; 78:178–91.

Buckner RL and Vincent JL. (2007). Unrest at rest: default activity and spontaneous network correlations. *Neuroimage.* Oct 1; 37(4):1091–6.

Burkhouse KL, Jacobs RH, Peters AT, Ajilore O, Watkins ER, and Langenecker SA. (2017). Neural correlates of rumination in adolescents with remitted major depressive disorder and healthy controls. *Cogn Affect Behav Neurosci.* Apr; 17(2):394–405.

Cavézian C, Danckert J, Lerond J, Daléry J, d'Amato T, and Saoud M. (2007). Visual-perceptual abilities in healthy controls, depressed patients, and schizophrenia patients. *Brain Cogn.* Aug; 64(3):257–64.

Chatterjee A. (1994). Picturing unilateral spatial neglect: viewer versus object centered reference frames. *J Neurol Neurosurg Psychiatry.* Oct; 57(10):1236–40.

Chatterjee A, Maher LM, and Heilman KM. (1995). Spatial characteristics of thematic role representation. *Neuropsychologia.* May;33(5):643–8.

Claunch JD, Falchook AD, Williamson JB, Fischler I, Jones EM, Baum JB, and Heilman KM. (2012). Famous faces but not remembered spaces influence vertical line bisections. *J Clin Exp Neuropsychol.* 34(9):919–24.

Coren S. (1995). Differences in divergent thinking as a function of handedness and sex. *Am J Psychol.* 108(3): 311–25.

Corkin SS. (1968). Acquisition of motor skill after bilateral medial temporal-lobe excision. *Neuropsychologia.* 6: 255–65.

Cuellar-Partida G, Tung JY, Eriksson N, Albrecht E, et al. (2021). Genome-wide association study identifies 48 common genetic variants associated with handedness. *Nat Hum Behav.* Jan;5(1):59–70.

Davidson RJ, Schwartz GE, Saron C, Bennett J, and Goldman DJ. (1979). Frontal versus parietal EEG asymmetry during positive and negative affect. *Psychophysiology.* 16:202–3.

Denny K. (2009). Handedness and evidence from a large population survey. *Laterality.* May;14(3):246–55.

Denny-Brown D. (1958). The nature of apraxia. *J Nerv Ment Dis.* 126(1):9–32.

Denny-Brown D and Chambers RA. (1958). The parietal lobe and behavior. *Res Publ Assoc Res Nerv Ment Dis.* 36:35–117.

Denny-Brown D, Meyer JS, and Horenstein S. (1952). The significance of perceptual rivalry resulting from parietal lesions. *Brain.* 75:434–71.

Drago V, Heilman KM, and Foster PS. (2010). Feeling down: idiom or nature? *J Neuropsychiatry Clin Neurosci.* Summer;22(3):338–44.

Dunn RT, Kimbrell TA, Ketter TA, Frye MA, Willis MW, Luckenbaugh DA, and Post RM. (2002). Principal components of the Beck Depression Inventory and regional cerebral metabolism in unipolar and bipolar depression. *Biol Psychiatry.* Mar 1;51(5):387–99.

Epstein J, Pan H, Kocsis JH, Yang Y, Butler T, Chusid J, Hochberg H, Murrough J, Strohmayer E, Stern E, and Silbersweig DA. (2006). Lack of ventral striatal response to positive stimuli in depressed versus normal subjects. *Am J Psychiatry.* Oct;163(10):1784–90.

Ergun-Marterer A, Ergun E, Mentes M, and Oder W. (2001). Altitudinal neglect in a patient with occipital infarction. *Brain Inj.* Apr;15(4):363–70.

Faurie C and Raymond M. (2004). Handedness frequency over more than ten thousand years. *Proc Biol Sci.* Feb 7;271(Suppl 3):S43–5.

Fink GR, Halligan PW, Marshall JC, Frith CD, Frackowiak RS, and Dolan RJ. (1996). Where in the brain does visual attention select the forest and the trees? *Nature.* Aug 15;382(6592):626–8.

Fogassi L, Gallese V, Buccino G, Craighero L, Fadiga L, and Rizzolatti G. (2001). Cortical mechanism for the visual guidance of hand grasping movements in the monkey: a reversible inactivation study. *Brain*. Mar;124(Pt 3):571–86.

Folstein MF, Folstein SE, and McHugh PR. (1975). "Mini-mental state". A practical method for grading the cognitive state of patients for the clinician. *J Psychiatr Res*. Nov;12(3):189–98.

Forsman LJ, de Manzano O, Karabanov A, Madison G, and Ullén F. (2012). Differences in regional brain volume related to the extraversion-introversion dimension—a voxel based morphometry study. *Neurosci Res*. Jan;72(1):59–67.

Foundas AL, Hong K, Leonard CN, and Heilman KM. (1996). The human primary motor cortex. *Neurology*. May; 46(5):1491–2.

Frijda NH. (2016). The evolutionary emergence of what we call "emotions". *Cogn Emot*. 30(4):609–20.

Gainotti G. (1972). Emotional behavior and hemispheric side of lesion. *Cortex*. 8:41–55.

Gasparrini WG, Spatz P, Heilman KM, and Coolidge FL. (1978). Hemispheric asymmetries of affective processing as determined by the Minnesota multiphasic personality inventory. *J Neurol Neurosurg Psychiatry*. 41:470–3.

Geschwind N and Kaplan E. (1962). A human cerebral deconnection syndrome. A preliminary report. *Neurology*. Oct;12:675–85.

Goldberg ME and Bushnell MC. (1981). Behavioral enhancement of visual responses in monkey cerebral cortex. II. Modulation in frontal eye fields specifically related to saccades. *J Neurophysiol*. Oct;46(4):773–87.

Goldstein K. (1948). *Language and Language Disturbances*. New York: Grune and Stratton.

Goodglass H and Kaplan E. (1963). Disturbance of gesture and pantomime in aphasia. *Brain*. 86:703–20.

Hamann S, Monarch ES, and Goldstein FC. (2002). Impaired fear conditioning in Alzheimer's disease. *Neuropsychologia*. 40(8):1187–95. doi: 10.1016/s0028-3932(01) 00223-8.

Hecaen H, Ajuriagurra J, and de Massonet J. (1951). Les troubles visuoconstuctifs par lesion parieto-occipitale droit. *Encephale*. 40:122–79.

Heilman KM. (1979). Neglect and related syndromes. In KM Heilman and E Valenstein (Eds.), *Clinical Neuropsychology*. New York: Oxford University Press. pp. 243–293.

Heilman KM. (1997). The neurobiology of emotional experience. *J Neuropsychiatry Clin Neurosci*. Summer;9(3):439–48.

Heilman KM and Rothi, LJG. (2012). Apraxia. In KM Heilman and E Valenstein (Eds.), *Clinical Neuropsychology*, 5th edition. New York: Oxford University Press, pp. 214–37.

Heilman KM, Schwartz HD, and Geschwind N. (1975). Defective motor learning in ideomotor apraxia. *Neurology*. Nov;25(11):1018–20.

Heilman KM, Schwartz H, and Watson RT. (1978). Hypoarousal in patients with the neglect syndrome and emotional indifference. *Neurology*. 28:229–32.

Heilman KM and Van Den Abell T. (1979). Right hemisphere dominance for mediating cerebral activation. *Neuropsychologia*. 17(3–4):315–21.

Heilman KM, Watson RT and Valenstein, E. (2012). Neglect and related disorders. In KM Heilman and E Valenstein (Eds.), *Clinical Neuropsychology*, 5th edition. New York: Oxford University Press, pp. 296–348.

Hicks RA and Pellegrini RJ. (1978). Handedness and anxiety. *Cortex*. Mar;14(1):119–21.

Hillis AE, Melissa N, Heidler J, Barker PB, Herskovits EH, and Degaonkar M. (2005). Anatomy of spatial attention: insights from perfusion imaging and hemispatial neglect in acute stroke. *Neurosci*. Mar 23;25(12):3161–7.

Ikemoto S and Panksepp J. (1999). The role of nucleus accumbens dopamine in motivated behavior: a unifying interpretation with special reference to reward-seeking. *Brain Res Rev.* 31:6–41.

Jeerakathil TJ and Kirk A. (1994). A representational vertical bias. *Neurology.* Apr;44(4):703–6.

Jewell G and McCourt M. (2000). Pseudoneglect: a review and meta-analysis of performance factors in line bisection tasks. *Neuropsychologia.* 38(1):93–110.

Kaiser RH, Andrews-Hanna JR, Wager TD, and Pizzagalli DA. (2015). Large-scale network dysfunction in major depressive disorder: a meta-analysis of resting-state functional connectivity. *JAMA Psychiatr y.* Jun;72(6):603–11.

Katrin K, Schlaug G, Schleicher A, Steinmetz H, Dabringhaus A, Roland PE, and Zilles K. (1996). Asymmetry in the human motor cortex and handedness. *NeuroImage.* Dec;4(30):216–22.

Króliczak G, Piper BJ, and Frey SH. (2016). Specialization of the left supramarginal gyrus for hand-independent praxis representation is not related to hand dominance. *Neuropsychologia.* Dec;93(Pt B):501–12. doi: 10.1016/j.neuropsychologia.2016.03.023.

Laland KN. (2008). Exploring gene-culture interactions: insights from handedness, sexual selection and niche-construction case studies. *Philos Trans R Soc Lond B Biol Sci.* Nov;363(1509):3577–89.

Lawrence DG and Kuypers HGJM. (1968). The functional organization of the motor system in the monkey. *Brain.* 91:15–36.

LeMay M. (1977). Asymmetries of the skull and handedness. Phrenology revisited. *J Neurol Sci.* Jun;32(2):243–53.

Lhermitte F. (1983). Utilization behavior and its relation to lesions of the frontal lobes. *Brain.* 106(2):237–55.

Liepmann H. (1908/2001). Agnosic disorders (1908) [classical article]. *Cortex.* Sep;37(4): 547–53.

Liepmann H. (1920). Apraxia. *Ergbn Ges Med.* 1:516–43.

Lissauer H. (1890). Ein Fall von Seelenblindheit Nebst Einem Beitrage zur Theori derselben. *Archiv fur Psychiatrie und Nervenkrankheiten.* 21:222–70.

Mańkowska A, Harciarek M, and Heilman KM. (2020). Depressive symptoms on the allocation of vertical attention. *Cogn Behav Neurol.* Jun;33(2):137–44.

Mańkowska A, Heilman KM, Williamson JB, and Harciarek M. (2018). Age-related changes in the allocation of vertical attention. *J Int Neuropsychol Soc.* Nov;24(10):1121–4.

McCourt ME and Jewell G. (1999). Visuospatial attention in line bisection: stimulus modulation of pseudoneglect. *Neuropsychologia.* 37(7):843–55.

Medina J, Kannan V, Pawlak MA, Kleinman JT, Newhart M, Davis C, Heidler-Gary JE, Herskovits EH, and Hillis AE. (2009). Neural substrates of visuospatial processing in distinct reference frames: evidence from unilateral spatial neglect. *J Cogn Neurosci.* Nov;21(11):2073–84.

Mesulam MM. (1981). A cortical network for directed attention and unilateral neglect. *Ann Neurol* Oct;10(4):30

McManus IC, Davison A, Armour JA. (2013) Multilocus genetic models of handedness closely resemble single-locus models in explaining family data and are compatible with genome-wide association studies. *Ann NY Acad Sci.* 1288(1):48–58.

Milner B. (1962). Laterality effects in audition. In VB Mountcastle (Ed.), *Interhemispheric Relations and Cerebral Dominance.* Baltimore: Johns Hopkins University Press, pp. 177–95.

Mori E and Yamadori A. (1989). Rejection behaviour: a human homologue of the abnormal behaviour of Denny-Brown and Chambers' monkey with bilateral parietal ablation. *J Neurol Neurosurg Psychiatry.* Nov;52(11):1260–6.

Moruzzi G and Magoun HW. (1949). Brain stem reticular formation and activation of the EEG. *Electroencephalogr Clin Neurophysiol.* Nov;1(4):455–73.

Newland GA. (1981). Differences between left- and right-handers on a measure of creativity. *Percept Mot Ski.* 53(3):787–92.

Nirkko AC, Ozdoba C, Redmond SM, Bürki M, Schroth G, Hess CW, and Wiesendanger M. (2001). Different ipsilateral representations for distal and proximal movements in the sensorimotor cortex: activation and deactivation patterns. *Neuroimage.* May;13(5):825–35.

Okun MS, Bowers D, Springer U, Shapira N, Malone D, Rezai AR, Nuttin B, Heilman KM, Morecraft RJ, Rasmussen S, Greenberg BD, Foote KD, and Goodman WK. (2004). What's in a "smile?" Intra-operative observations of contralateral smiles induced by deep brain stimulation. *Neurocase.* Aug;10(4):271–9.

Olds J and Milner P. (1954). Positive reinforcement produced by electrical stimulation of septal area and other regions of rat brain. *J Comp Physiol Psychol.* Dec;47(6):419–27.

Osgood CE, Suci GJ, and Tanenbaum PH. *The Measurement of Meaning.* Urbana: University of Illinois Press.

Pardo JV, Fox PT, and Raichle ME. (1991). Localization of a human system for sustained attention by positron emission tomography. *Nature.* Jan 3;349(6304):61–4.

Penfield W and Flanigin H. (1950). Surgical therapy of temporal lobe seizures. *AMA Arch Neurol Psychiatry.* Oct;64(4):491–500.

Perani D, Vallar G, Paulesu E, Alberoni M, and Fazio F. (1993). Left and right hemisphere contribution to recovery from neglect after right hemisphere damage—an [18F]FDG pet study of two cases. *Neuropsychologia.* Feb;31(2):115–25.

Phelps ME, Mazziotta JC, Baxter L, and Gerner R. (1984). Positron emission tomographic study of affective disorders: problems and strategies. *Ann Neurol.* 15(Suppl):S149–56.

Pitzalis S, Spinelli D, and Zoccolotti P. (1997). Vertical neglect: behavioral and electrophysiological data. *Cortex.* Dec;33(4):679–88.

Poizner H, Mack L, Verfaellie M, Rothi LJG, and Heilman KM. (1990). Three-dimensional computer graphic analysis of apraxia. *Brain.* 113:85–101.

Raichle ME, MacLeod AM, Snyder AZ, Powers WJ, Gusnard DA, and Shulman GL. (2001). A default mode of brain function. *Proc Natl Acad Sci U S A.* Jan 16;98(2):676–82.

Ramos Bernardes da Silva Filho S, Oliveira Barbosa JH, Rondinoni C, Carlos Dos Santos A, Garrido Salmon CE, Kilza da Costa Lima N, Ferriolli E, and Moriguti JC. (2017). Neurodegeneration profile of Alzheimer's patients: a brain morphometry study. *Neuroimage Clin.* Apr 3;15:15–24.

Ramos-Brieva JA, Olivan J, Palomares A, and Vela A. (1984). Is there right hemisphere dysfunction in major depression? *Int J Neurosci.* Apr;23(2):103–9.

Rapcsak SZ, Cimino CR, and Heilman KM. (1998). Altitudinal neglect. *Neurology.* Feb;38(2):277–81.

Robinson RG and Starkstein SE. (1989). Mood disorders following stroke: new findings and future directions. *J Geriatr Psychiatry.* 22(1):1–15.

Roig M and Cicero F. (1994). Hemisphericity style, sex, and performance on a line-bisection task: an exploratory study. *Percept Mot Ski.* Feb;78(1):115–20.

Rossi GS and Rodadini G. (1967). Experimental analysis of cerebral dominance in man. In C Millikan and FL Darley (Eds.), *Brain Mechanisms Underlying Speech and Language.* New York: Grune and Stratton. pp. 167–184.

Rothi LJG, Mack L, Verfaellie M., Brown P, and Heilman KM. (1988). Ideomotor apraxia: error pattern analysis. *Aphasiology.* 2:381–7.

Sackeim HA, Gur RC, and Saucy MC. (1978). Emotions are expressed more intensely on the left side of the face. *Science.* Oct 27;202(4366):434–6.

Schrandt NJ, Tranel D, and Damasio H. (1989). The effects of total cerebral lesions on skin response to signal stimuli. *Neurology*. 39(Suppl 1):223.

Seashore C. (1919). Seashore Tests of Musical Ability. *The Psychology of Musical Talent*. Silver, Burdett & Company.

Segundo JP, Naquet R, and Buser P. (1955). Effects of cortical stimulation on electro-cortical activity in monkeys. *J Neurophysiol*. 18(3):236–45.

Sheline YI, Barch DM, Price JL, Rundle MM, Vaishnavi SN, Snyder AZ, Mintun MA, Wang S, Coalson RS, and Raichle ME. (2009). The default mode network and self-referential processes in depression. *PNAS*. Feb 10;106(6):1942–7.

Shelton PA, Bowers D, and Heilman KM. (1990). Peripersonal and vertical neglect. *Brain*. Feb;113(Pt 1):191–205.

Shenal BV, Hinze S, and Heilman KM. (2012). The cost of action miscues: hemispheric asymmetries. *Brain Cogn*. Jun;79(1):45–8.

Sicotte NL, Woods RP, and Mazziotta JC. (1999). Handedness in twins: a meta-analysis. *Laterality*. Jul;4(3):265–86.

Stuss DT and Benson DF. (1986). *The Frontal Lobes*. New York: Raven Press.

Suavansri K, Falchook AD, Williamson JB, and Heilman KM. (2012). Right up there: hemispatial and hand asymmetries of altitudinal pseudoneglect. *Brain Cogn*. Aug;79(3):216–20.

Szpak A, Thomas N, and Nicholls M. (2016). Hemispheric asymmetries in perceived depth revealed through a radial line bisection task. *Exp Brain Res*. 234:807–13.

Taylor HG and Heilman KM. (1980). Left-hemisphere motor dominance in right handers. *Cortex*. Dec;16(4):587–603.

Terzian H. (1964). Behavioral and EEG effects of intracarotid sodium amytal injections. *Acta Neurochirurgica (Vienna)*. 12:230–40.

Tucker DM. (1981). Lateral brain function, emotion and conceptualization. *Psychol Bull*. 89:19–46.

Tucker DM and Williamson PA. (1984). Asymmetric neural control in human self-regulation. *Psychol Rev*. 91:185–215.

Uc EY, Rizzo M, Anderson SW, Shi Q, and Dawson JD. (2006). Unsafe rear-end collision avoidance in Alzheimer's disease. *J Neurol Sci*. Dec 21;251(1–2):35–43.

Ungerleider L and Mishkin M. (1982). Contribution of striate inputs to the visuospatial functions of parieto-preoccipital cortex in monkeys. *Behav Brain Res*. Sep;6(1):57–77.

van Wingen GA, Tendolkar I, Urner M, van Marle HJ, Denys D, Verkes RJ, and Fernández G. (2014). Short-term antidepressant administration reduces default mode and task-positive network connectivity in healthy individuals during rest. *Neuroimage*. Mar;88:47–53.

Verfaellie M and Heilman KM. (1990). Hemispheric asymmetries in attentional control: implications for hand preference in sensorimotor tasks. *Brain Cogn*. Sep;14(1):70–80.

Watson RT and Heilman KM. (1983). Callosal apraxia. *Brain*. Jun;106 (Pt 2):391–403.

Watson RT, Heilman KM, Miller BD, and King FA. (1974). Neglect after mesencephalic reticular formation lesions. *Neurology*. Mar;24(3):294–8.

Watson RT, Miller BD, and Heilman KM. (1978). Nonsensory neglect. *Ann Neurol*. Jun;3(6):505–8.

Watson RT, Valenstein E, and Heilman KM. (1981). Thalamic neglect. Possible role of the medial thalamus and nucleus reticularis in behavior. *Arch Neurol*. Aug;38(8):501–6.

Williamson JB, Drago V, Harciarek M, Falchook AD, Wargovich BA, and Heilman KM. (2019). Chronological effects of emotional valence on the self-selected retrieval of autobiographical memories. *Cogn Behav Neurol*. Mar;32(1):11–15.

Wright CI, Williams D, Feczko E, Barrett LF, Dickerson BC, Schwartz CE, and Wedig MM. (2006). Neuroanatomical correlates of extraversion and neuroticism. *Cereb Cortex.* Dec;16(12):1809–19.

Yerkes RM and Dodson JD. (1908). The relation of strength to rapidity of habituation. *J Comp Neurol Psychol.* 18:459–82.

Yokoyama K, Jennings R, Ackles P, Hood P, and Boller F. (1987). Lack of heart rate changes during an attention-demanding task after right hemisphere lesions. *Neurology.* Apr;37(4):624–30. Erratum in: *Neurology* 1987 May;37(5):748.

INDEX

Note: Page numbers in *italics* indicate figures on the corresponding pages.

Printed in Great Britain
by Amazon